LOVING Says It All

by

Norman Pittenger

THE PILGRIM PRESS
New York/Philadelphia

Library of Congress Cataloging in Publication Data

Pittenger, William Norman, 1905-
Loving says it all.

1. Christian ethics—Anglican authors.
2. Process theology. I. Title.
BJ1251.P57 241'.03 78-5671
ISBN 0-8298-0352-1

The Pilgrim Press, 287 Park Avenue South, New York, New York 10010

For Michael Till, Dean of Chapel,
King's College, Cambridge:
fellow-priest, devoted colleague,
and beloved friend

Contents

Preface

This book is an attempt to open up and explore, in a suggestive fashion, some of the ethical implications of a Christian perspective understood in the light of process thought. It adopts a Christian perspective because it assumes the central affirmation of Christian faith: the basic reality in the cosmos is Love, self-disclosed in the world and given supreme focus in the event of Jesus Christ. It is a perspective that is understood in terms of "process": that is, God, the world, and humankind are taken to be in movement, dynamic rather than static, societal in nature, with "becoming" given priority over "being." And my concern is with the specifically ethical implications of such a perspective, so understood, since this is an area where a good deal of hard thinking is needed and where the position I have taken is likely to have much to offer.

One reason for this conviction has been well stated by Prof. James E. Griffiss in an essay in *The Anglican Theological Review* (Spring 1973), in which he writes about just such a position:

> Man is a personality in the making, one in whom creativity and freedom find their expression in the process of his entering into relationships with others—at any level of transcendence, human or divine. The social, communal relationships of human beings with one another and ultimately with God are characterized by a process of growth and development through which a person discovers his own potential to live responsibly in freedom. His fundamental ontology or nature can only be

> defined in the context of that process—as it is being realized or as it is not—through his openness to the possibility of love. Hence man's activity—whether sexual or otherwise—can be described as "natural" not because it conforms to an already determined human nature . . . but because it is "in accord with the best direction for the fulfillment of human personality."

Professor Griffiss goes on to say:

> Man's ontology, in his existence as a creature of God, is that he is called into relationship, ultimately in the *humanitas* itself, particularly in a variety of social, communal structures through which he is able to understand and develop his personhood. . . . Man's call to love stands as the basic theological category: it is prior to anything else that may be said about him. It is finally grace, that is, a gift, a freely bestowed favour. (Ibid., p. 232)

I quote these words not because their writer kindly says that my book *Making Sexuality Human* (New York: The Pilgrim Press, 1970) is "the most interesting theologically" of recent works on the subject of human sexuality, but because it seems to me that what I have here reproduced is an admirable summary of a position that enables us to make an important fresh start in our effort to grasp the significance of humanity's ethical "project" and hence come to a better understanding of what another writer, Prof. Anthony Quinton, has called "the more or less enduring system of tastes, propensities, desires and aversions, values and habits which constitute the inner causes or determinants of conduct" (*Times Literary Supplement* [London], July 27, 1973, p. 873). For it is indubitably true that conduct, an individual's ethical life in its broadest sense, is determined precisely by such "tastes, propensities, desires and aversions, values and habits"; and from a Christian perspective these are, or ought to be, grounded in love of the kind or quality that is revealed in the event of Christ as basic to the cosmos itself.

In my attempt to work through this, I shall begin by some discussion of the ethical perspective itself, moving on from that to show how the Christian insistence on Love (as God's nature and humankind's intended nature) is related to this perspective. Next I shall consider some of the consequences of this double view, asking what in fact it implies for ethical norms or principles. The succeeding chapters will concern themselves with the important question of "absolute" and "relative" in ethical matters; the place of "situation" and "context," two recently proposed factors in all moral decision; and the practical application of our entire discussion, with attention to human sexuality, on the one hand, and social relationships such as those obtaining in political and economic life, on the other, both taken as examples of a general way of looking at and working with the central norm of fulfillment in love of person in society.

I do not for a moment think that this book is an exhaustive or adequate discussion of matters so important in our own and in every period of history. As I remarked at the beginning of this preface, I am seeking only to "open up and explore, in a suggestive fashion" what contribution a Christian process attitude may make to the perennial problem of humanity's existence and behavior as ethical beings. It is my hope that what is here written may provide, so to speak, a first step; it is for others to carry on the work, if they think it worth doing.

It remains for me to thank many friends and colleagues in the Faculty of Divinity of the University of Cambridge for the help they have given me in conversation and above all through the meetings of the "D Society"—a Cambridge senior group that meets fortnightly each term to study together matters of interest in philosophy of religion, moral philosophy, and theology. These chapters were given first as lectures to a group in St. Louis, Missouri, in March 1974, arranged by Dr. R.F. Tombaugh, to whom I am much indebted. I would also like to express my gratitude to the faculty and members of the Institute for Religion and Human Development at the Texas

Medical Center in Houston, Texas, where I spent a happy and highly profitable three weeks in 1974 and where much of our discussion centered on the very issues treated in this book. For any faults in that which I have written, I alone am responsible.

Norman Pittenger
King's College
Cambridge, England

1

The Ethical Question in a Process Perspective

1

The Ethical Question in a Process Perspective

The ethical question—or the question of ethics.

I have used the word ethics and its adjective, rather than the words morality and morals, because I wish to consider in this book the fundamental issues concerning the grounds or the bases for human moral behavior. In other words, the matter under discussion will be the way in which, and the sense in which, we may state meaningfully the fact that people are able to act responsibly as living, developing creatures who are aware of ethical principles. Traditionally, morality has to do with the understanding of the proper ethical norms and the conduct which follows upon that understanding. Ethics is a prior study, its interest being in the assumptions that make it possible for morality to exist in any sense. It is with that prior matter that we shall concern ourselves.

In the second place, I have put in the title of this opening chapter the words "in a process perspective." These words indicate my own conviction, for which I shall argue in what follows, that only when we see people, and their interest in ethical principles, in terms of "becoming"—of moving toward ends or goals or a "subjective aim" which they appropriate and for which they decide—can we make much sense of their ethical awareness. When we think of ourselves in static terms, as "beings" who are (so to speak) finished articles and who can adequately be defined in language appropriate to such, we are deluding ourselves *and* we are interpreting ethical principles in a fashion that is itself static and incapable of accounting for the obvious development of those principles during the history of the human race.

This is no place to embark on a history of human ethical awareness during the long period from first-recorded primitive days to the present. Nor should I wish it thought that I am competent to undertake such a daunting task. But one thing is quite clear. The ways in which ethical principles have been seen, equally with the ways in which response has been made to them, have changed enormously during the three or four thousand years about which we have any certain knowledge. Through the greater part of that long story, indeed until fairly recently, the assumption has been that when we say humankind we are speaking of beings who have remained and remain just about the same, the finished article to which reference was made above. In different ways, of course, yet nonetheless with almost monotonous regularity, men and women have been regarded as having been created pretty much as they now are. And when careful attention has been paid to their sense of ethical obligation, it has been done fairly consistently under the assumption that for such a "finished" being ethical obligation will manifest itself in an equally static fashion.

It is admitted, of course, that there has been development in the profundity of insight with which such ethical obligation has been understood. On my part I should agree that there has been a continued recognition of precisely such a sense of obligation, expressed in varying ways at different times: "ought" seems to have been an accompaniment of human experience from earliest days. Yet precisely because the concept of human nature remained fixed, and fixed in a world which itself also was thought to have been created in an equally "finished" manner, the whole question of ethics has been looked at as an effort to discover the eternally abiding laws that are thought to be inevitably present whenever people are talked about as beings aware of an "ought."

A static view of humankind, a static view of the world, and a static view of ethical principles—these three have gone together. And I may here also add, a static view of God. Put in the simplest way, the idea has been that an immutable, unchanging deity, entirely perfect in every respect, has created a world that is also completed in its main structures. In that world, God has created humankind with such-and-such a nature. And for humankind there have been revealed or given such-and-such immutable laws according to which people are to live—although, alas, very often people have not done this and hence have been guilty of unethical conduct for which they must assume responsibility.

Broadly, that is the picture which we have inherited. But once people learned that the world was not created in any such completed fashion and that human beings themselves are the product of a long series of changes and by no means simply identical with their own past, this picture broke down. Knowledge of evolution in its narrower biological sense and evolution in its wider significance of development cosmically and physically, as well as psychologically and sociologically, has altered things. Our ethical understanding, however, has continued to be based upon the earlier picture; therefore it does not fit in with what we now know and accept in a more general sense. This, I take it, is the reason for what nowadays is regarded by many as the collapse of ethics: the so-called loss of all sense of morality, and the great confusion felt in so many quarters about "ought," about ethical principles, and about *any* valid perspective on human duty and responsibility.

Consequently, it is widely assumed that we have only a simple choice between two possibilities. *Either* we give up ethics altogether and talk simply about conventional notions—in the sense of customary, accepted at a given period and place—of what constitutes "the good life" and the human behavior patterns appropriate to it. *Or* we "return" to supposedly abiding laws, changeless in essence and adapted to a human nature that is supposedly equally changeless. The former expresses itself in the complete relativism thought by many to mark any "open" or "permissive" society, a society which almost by definition (as it is thought) must be unprincipled; sometimes there is an attempt to extract from the fact of evolution, as we have come to understand it, some broad ethical principle like "survival"—but with no enduring vision of what is *truly good*. The latter —the "return" motif—shows itself in repeated appeals to our contemporaries that they should go back to "the good old ways," to the dictates commonly accepted in earlier ages, to "our traditional ethical codes," and so on.

Neither of these alternatives seems to me desirable; certainly the second of them is almost, if not entirely, impossible. On the one hand, change in and of itself is simply a descriptive statement—things do not continue as they were. Certainly that is true enough; but it does not provide us with any insight into what principles may be worth preserving not because they happen to be ancient but because they are in some fashion enduringly important for humankind with the sense of "ought." On the other hand, if anything is clear to us it is that we cannot "return" to the past when this signifies only the *repetition* of that past. James Russell Lowell put the case in familiar words when in his poem "The Present Crisis" he spoke about how "new occasions teach new duties" and went on to affirm that "time makes ancient good uncouth." Change is indeed a fact; we live in it and we are part of it—and that makes it abundantly plain that those who live in changed conditions, under different skies so to speak, are not able to reverse the way things have gone and live as if nothing had happened to us and to our knowledge of the world and of ourselves.

But there may be a third path. That path would recognize fully the fact of change, the priority of "becoming" over "being," and the way in which human beings are creatures who live in and, what is more, *are*, a history. In other words, it would accept a "process perspective." At the same time, however, it would affirm that there is a general direction of advance in the process, and it would argue that for humanity there is a growing awareness of where that direction points. Since human beings are essentially—or, rather, existentially—a movement from potentiality toward actuality, from possibility to realization through responsible decisions made in such freedom as is theirs, the enduring ethical principles will be those that best enable just such actualization or realization. One's vocation as a human being is to become what it is in him or her to become: *a person*, a human being in relationship with kindred beings, a human being who "ought" so to live and act as to promote exactly that personhood-in-relationship. This third path is perfectly possible as an option; its merit is that it does not ask the *impossible* by urging any "returns," save for such "expert testimony" as our ancestors can give us about how *they* sought to achieve the realization or actualization of which I have spoken. Nor does it assume that simply because there is constant change no direction can be discerned and we are the inevitable victims of mere flux. It accepts the fact of evolutionary development without succumbing to the idiotic notion that all process must be *progress* and that moral life is merely and only letting ourselves move with the tide, without principles of any sort.

Not only must we see humankind in a process perspective, but we must also grasp the societal quality of human existence. This was the point of the comments in the last paragraph about personhood-in-relationship. Many of us tend to think of ourselves as "individuals"; and that is true as far as it goes, in that we are instances of a general class or category, with certain common characteristics which we have come to call human. But a human being is an individual in a specific way: a human being is *one with others.* That is why we use the word person. A person is always with others; indeed, we could say that personality and sociality are two sides of the same coin so far as human beings are concerned.

For the ethical question, the sociality of humankind has the important consequence that the movement toward or away from the actualization of any one human being is inevitably also a contribution which that person makes for or against the actualization of other human beings. Either the choices and actions help that wider actualization, or they do not. As we shall see, this points toward one of those enduring ethical principles to which we have made reference earlier in this chapter. Personal and social patterns of behavior are interrelated. Hence, people who set out to be and do only what they want for themselves fail to act out their own existence; on the other hand, people who entirely abdicate their "selfhood" and become nothing more than one of the crowd have also failed to act out their own existence. When Aristotle followed his treatment of personal behavior by a discussion of humankind as *zoon politikon* (not political, but social, since *polis* for the Greek mind suggested sociality and not just what *we* call politics), he intimated this double quality of human life.

Self-awareness assures us that we have the capacity to *think* —that is to say, there can be no doubt that Boethius' definition of a human being as "an individual substance of a rational nature," which Thomas Aquinas took over, contains a genuine insight. The trouble with the definition, as with all similar definitions, is primarily in its morphological nature; it is interested in what might be called persisting structural qualities in humankind and misses the dynamic aspects on which we have insisted. But this capacity to think, and to think (as we might say) reasonably, must be coupled with an equally stressed capacity to *feel.* In fact, human existence is largely a matter of feelings. By this I do not intend merely emotional states, although these are real enough; I am trying to point to something much deeper than emotion, namely, the appreciative, valuational, aesthetic side of humanity. Poetry, music, art in its several forms—all are expressions of this human quality, not only on the part of those who create such things but also on the part of those who respond to them, "appreciate" them. Here too the social nature of humankind comes into the picture, since we relate ourselves to others in ways that are much deeper than rational awareness and understanding.

In the course of the evolutionary process, humankind has emerged as that level in the creation which strives toward fulfillment in a more or less self-conscious fashion, with some degree of rationality, with deep "feeling-tones," and with desires and yearnings that are inescapable and that carry with them either the joy of attainment or the sadness of failure of such attainment. All this, I urge, needs to be taken into our reckoning when we consider human beings as ethical animals. A person's sense of "ought" speaks to the whole of what he or she is, not only to a single part or aspect. In the dynamic forward thrust, for better or for worse, a person thinks and feels, strives and desires, and belongs with others; a person moves in the direction of becoming what his or her possibilities suggest, or moves in the opposite direction, frustrating self-actualization and thus suffering from what might appropriately be styled human diminishment.

Finally, we see in ourselves and observe in others an ability to engage ourselves, commit ourselves, or give ourselves to projects or purposes or causes that for one reason or another make their appeal or seem good and worthy. The existentialists have especially laid emphasis on this "engagement"—rightly so, since one who has no "project" to be devoted to is hardly human in his or her real integrity. To this we shall return at a later stage.

I have spoken of the sense of "ought" which seems to be ineradicable in humankind. This sense has been described and explained in many different ways, but perhaps we can sum up its meaning in two familiar statements. One is from Immanuel

Kant, with his talk about "the categorical imperative." By this Kant was pointing to a feeling that is widespread, indeed, universal: *I must do my duty*. But exactly what is that duty and what are its contents? Here we have our problem, for obviously these are very largely conditioned by the situations in which people find themselves, by the society of which they are a part, by inherited notions about how best to behave and what choices are best to make. The content of duty among, say, South Sea Islanders a hundred years ago will be different from that found today in Britain or the United States. Even in Western culture the content will not be identical in Italy and in Ireland. Nonetheless, a sense that duty *is* to be done seems to be pervasive in all cultures and societies.

What is the origin of this categorical imperative? Some writers have tried to show that it is based upon a need for security of the sort that relates the individual to his or her tribe or group. Others think that it is psychologically explicable as an internalizing of the social patterns or the particular prejudices communicated by parents or other controlling figures—the *superego* of Freud is such an internalized "conscience" with its actual origin in parental or social commands. In my judgment, these and other attempts to show the origins of the sense of "ought" succeed only in telling us in a descriptive sense the way in which this or that person, in this or that culture, comes to be *aware of* "ought"; it does not reduce this sense of "ought" to "nothing but" some particular social or psychological, or even physiological, cause. The problem here is in the very prevalent "nothing but" fallacy, Of course, there must be some way in which this sense comes into the realm of conscious awareness; but to describe what that way is does not negate the reality of the sense of obligation.

The second of the statements mentioned above is found in Thomas Aquinas' discussion of "natural law," or the supposedly innate sense of morality found in human beings everywhere. Aquinas says that the minimal content of this natural law is that "we should avoid the evil and do the good." Once again, the imperative is present: *we should.* But what *is* the evil to be avoided and the good to be done? Here, as with Kant's categorical imperative, the content of the obligation quite obviously differs from time to time and from place to place. Aquinas speaks about this content in terms of the society that he knew, its accepted patterns, and the like—although in fairness to him it must be added that he is by no means uncritical in doing this. At the same time, in his effort to give a sound theoretical basis for his summary of the natural law, he uses the wider philosophical-theological scheme that he believed to be correct. This involved the view that there is an "eternal law" which is the nature of God and that this eternal law is imparted to human creatures in the very fact of humanness, so that they have knowledge, however dim or vague, of how *naturally* they will live—"naturally" in that this will be in accordance with their own natures as human beings created in the image of God. Deviation from that natural law is wrong. What is required is a deepening of human awareness of both the "natural" habits of behavior, which are "virtues," and the "unnatural" habits, which are "vices." And the latter, of course, fall into the general category of "sins." Finally, the deliverances of the natural law are both confirmed and augmented by "positive law," more particularly when this is embodied in commandments taken to be revealed by God, but also (in some derivative sense) in the humanly achieved ethical systems that promote, indeed make possible, the continuation of human society in a peaceful and proper fashion.

In both Kant and Aquinas we have at least a serious reckoning with the presence of the "ought" that is the basis of all ethical discussion, even if the particular attempts made by each man to show how and why this sense is valid may not appeal to us. Here too there would seem to be a third path. Could it not be the case that in all human experience there is an awareness, however vaguely this is felt, that there is what Alfred North

Whitehead styled some "rightness" in things—in other words, an intuition of how the universe *goes*? Obviously it does not always *seem* that it goes in a particular way; there is conflicting evidence, so far as external and observable fact is concerned. Nonetheless, if human beings are emergents from the cosmos, it is at least conceivable that they are related to it in such a fashion that deep down inside people there is some indelible and ineradicable feeling that when and as they are living in accordance with the basic thrust of that cosmos (whatever this may be) they are living aright—and that they *ought* to live in such accordance with the basic thrust.

Now to talk in this way brings us close to a religious interpretation of "oughtness." We must turn in our next chapter to a further discussion of such a religious interpretation. Here we need only remark that the feeling of "ought" may very well be linked to human growth in a direction that will fulfill and not frustrate the proper actualization of possibility. And if the cosmos is, so to speak, on the side of that enterprise—an enterprise that emerges from it and that is also part of it—then we can accept the insight in the natural-law notion of ethical responsibility as correct, even if its particular scholastic (or Thomistic) formulation is not necessarily the right one. Somehow or other, the human sense of "ought" carries with it a feeling that "this is the way things go," however confused and inchoate the evidence may be.

Primitive people will think about this in primitive terms, talking of spirits at work in the world and present in this or that place; more sophisticated people will naturally have more sophisticated ways of seeing the matter. But I believe that Prof. John Macquarrie is correct when in his *Three Issues in Ethics* (London: SCM, 1970) he argues for a common factor running through all human ethical discernment. He is also correct, in my view, when in his more recently published book *The Concept of Peace* (London: SCM, 1973) he speaks of the possibility that "our human strivings towards a more authentically human life [are] borne up and supported by a reality beyond ourselves and even beyond human society in its totality," and goes on to describe this as "the experience of belonging to and working with a creative drive towards a wholeness and integrity that go beyond man's best aspirations" and show "a deep affinity between man and his ideals on the one hand and that vast nonhuman reality within which human life has its setting on the other" (p. 70).

As Professor Macquarrie rightly acknowledges, this is by no means a demonstrable assertion; yet it is certainly the case, as he urges, that in much contemporary thinking there is an increasing feeling that there is "an affinity" with a "wider reality" —a view that he finds expressed, although in a different context, in Barbara Johnson's and René Dubos' *Only One Earth* (New York: Penguin Books, 1972). The authors of this best-selling discussion of ecological issues tell us that the "intuitions" (as they call them) present in much traditional philosophy—that we were "part of a greater unity which transcends our local drives and needs"—are now being confirmed by plain scientific demonstration. Such intuitions, they say, "are factual descriptions of the way in which our universe actually works" (p. 85). In other words, we have the option, if nothing more, of believing that the best way to explain the basic sense of "ought" in human experience is through seeing this sense as a deep, if dim, awareness that the cosmos itself is on the side of humankind's forward thrust toward self-actualization in society.

I have just agreed that such a position is not demonstrable in any easy way. But it *is* an option, and it is a reasonable option too, since there is evidence for it, just as there is evidence for the other and negative view. This leads us to see that in ethical issues, above all in *the* ethical issue proposed by our sense of "oughtness," we are faced with the necessity for decision. We may, if we so wish, choose to believe that the entire cosmic story, including our own human existence, is nothing but "a tale told by an idiot, full of sound and fury, signifying nothing." On the other hand, we may choose to believe that despite so much that tells against our choice there is in the grain of the universe a strong backing for human fulfillment. Which of the two we choose will have a great deal to do with how we act. If we opt for *no* cosmic cooperation, then our behavior is bound to reflect our choice, although good manners, inherited notions of decency, and the like may avert the more outrageous expressions of it. But if we opt for cosmic cooperation, we will be inclined to behave in a manner that at least tries to bring about human self-realization in company with others.

As a matter of fact, the human race *has* opted for this latter position, as we can readily see if we take the long-range view. In very early days, this was done through what to us seem barbaric and absurd myths. As the centuries passed, more rational conceptions came into the picture. The Chinese talked about the fashion in which the "order of the heavens" and the "order of earth" were brought together in a great pattern of living. In Indian thought there was a belief that the basic ground of everything was also the deepest reality in human existence; and hence there was a correspondence between the cosmic structure as a whole and the structure of human life. In other cultures other ways were found to express the same insight. As we shall see in the next chapter, the Jewish-Christian development, reflected for us in the Old and New Testaments in the Bible, presents yet again a way in which "the stars in their courses" were believed to "fight with Sisera." In this view, the way the universe *really* goes, despite so much that seems contrary, is the way humanity *ought* to go; and not just because of an arbitrary fiat from on high but because there is a community between God and people. But of this more will be said later, and we must not anticipate our discussion of it.

It is significant that ordinary people talk of an "ought," and in their day-by-day natural and normal living assume that this "ought" is more than prejudice, personal or individual preference, or merely agreed-upon conventions. In some fashion, they imply by how they speak and act that the "ought" they feel is tied in with a drive they discern in the nature of things—this is the way things go and hence this is the way humankind "ought" to go.

How an "ought" can be grounded in an "is" has presented a great problem for philosophers concerned with ethical issues through the whole history of rational thought. Maybe it would have been better if attention had been paid not to the supposed "isness" that is behind "oughtness," but to the "coming to be," the "becoming," of a world that is in process. How best can we understand and portray that becoming; and in consequence, how can we relate such a cosmic becoming to the experienced reality of our own human becoming? If this approach were adopted, we should not be so much concerned with the maintenance of some status quo as with the possibilities of a movement toward what deep in our human consciousness we think of as a better situation.

That would not necessarily imply that in some automatic way everything is getting better; we have already urged that "process" is by no means identical with "progress." On the other hand, there might be—and for the most part men and women appear to assume that there is—a deep dynamic drive toward a more inclusive and widely shared good, in which they may have a place if they so decide. Furthermore, common experience indicates that for the most part men and women do take this to be the case and for this reason relate their sense of responsibility, the "ought" to which we have so often adverted, to the wider setting of our existence, or in religious language to *God*. That is why people talk about "doing God's will" and why sages with great insight have echoed Dante's words "In his will is our peace." But this again brings us close to the subject of the next chapter.

In our own time some sophisticated thinkers have argued that the only course for humankind, ethically speaking, is to *defy* the universe. So T.H. Huxley in a famous nineteenth-century lecture contrasted the cosmic process and human ethical aspirations. So too in more recent years, Bertrand Russell in his well-known essay "A Free Man's Worship" has said that human dignity consists in fighting against a meaningless world which has no purpose whatsoever. In thus fighting the world and asserting the "values" that humankind itself has set up as good and right, men and women are lonely and bound to be defeated, since death comes at the end of the struggle; yet Russell contends that it is better so to act, no matter what may be the conclusion of the matter. Here is a kind of stoicism, but one that dismisses the *anima mundi* or cosmic background which the original Stoics in the Greco-Roman Empire maintained was the ground for their interpretation of ethical principle.

But it is interesting that both Huxley and Russell, along with most other thoughtful people who speak or write in the same way, are still prepared to say that we "ought" to fight the cosmic process or defy the lifeless and indifferent forces in the world. Where did they get this notion of "ought"? They cannot tell us, since their position denies any source of ethical decision beyond the human one, even though they are not happy with simple acceptance of social conventions or accumulated prejudice as a clue to behavior. It is my belief that in their very denial of some moral grain in the universe they are using concepts and making demands that ultimately entail precisely such a moral quality in "how things go."

In any event, people of wisdom and compassion ought to welcome the fact that such defiance or negation of the cosmic process has not led those who adopt that stance to an utterly *un*-ethical position. This is why anybody who cares for other people must welcome the cooperation of humanists or agnostics in the continuing struggle to secure justice and peace in the world. Perhaps humanists and agnostics have unknowingly cut the ground out from under their own feet; nonetheless, their *practical* concern is on the side of the angels, if we may use the sort of language that such people would inevitably reject.

For our part, however, there is a conviction that ethical principles are so tied in with a world in process, where things are "coming to be," that we need to look very carefully at the religious perspective. We shall now do this; and our attention will focus on the manner in which that perspective with its ethical implications has developed in the Jewish-Christian tradition. This particular focus is chosen for two reasons. First, it is the one with which most readers of this book will have some familiarity, however slight and inadequate. Second, it is the one that I myself, along with a great many others even in this post-Christian age (as it is often called), regard as our best insight into the human situation, the human possibility, and the human ethical question.

2

The Ethical Question in a Christian Perspective

2

The Ethical Question in a Christian Perspective

The ethical question is inescapable for humankind. It cannot be avoided or evaded, however hard one may try. When one does try, the question appears again under some disguise. And as we have seen, the way in which the question is articulated is in some such terms as: What is my duty? What is my responsibility? What "ought" I to do or think or say? Basically what faces everyone is the "oughtness," and it is this with which one must somehow reckon.

In our own day the question is frequently discussed with no attention to its religious overtones or accompaniment. In an earlier time it was almost always otherwise; the ethical question and the religious question were inseparable in the thinking of most of the great writers on "oughtness." But for a variety of reasons, among them the widening gulf between what many think of as "religion" and the affairs of daily life, this intimate connection no longer obtains—at least in the circle of professional writers on the subject of ethics. It is not only that in some lands (notably Great Britain and the United States in recent years) analytic philosophy has tended to put religious discourse in an ambiguous position, although that philosophical movement unquestionably has had its influence. It is also the case that a large section of the public is alienated from its former cultural allegiance to religious ideas and practice.

It is my belief, as indicated in the preceding chapter, that quite apart from any consciously held religious convictions ethical questions *can be* and *are* raised; it is also my belief that it is possible to *discuss* these questions without immediately introducing such convictions. On the other hand, I am sure that a faithful following through of the ethical issue *does* raise profoundly religious issues. Indeed, I should be prepared to go further and say that the *basic* ethical question in back of and determining every specific consideration entails precisely what already we have urged: that the only possible authentication of the "ought" in human experience is to be found in a "rightness" in the universe itself. Otherwise, what is taken to be ethical is merely preferential behavior or conduct, engaged in because it happens to appeal to the persons in the situation; or it is only the reflection of the actually accepted patterns of expected behavior or conduct, whose sole justification is found in a desire to do what "everybody else" seems to be doing.

But how are we to envisage the religious position; or otherwise stated, what is the nature of the "rightness" in the universe that makes it possible meaningfully to say "ought" with respect to human conduct or behavior? Those of us who live in Europe, in Great Britain, on the American continents, and in those parts of the world where European civilization has had its influence are familiar with one specific religious tradition, the Christian one. This is one of the reasons for attention to that tradition in its ethical implications. Another is that for me, and doubtless for at least some of my readers, the essential affirmations of that Christian tradition constitute "the master-light of all our seeing." In one form or another, with whatever hesitations or doubts, we are prepared to call ourselves and to think of ourselves both as inheritors from that tradition and as committed to it. In other words, our perspective is bound to be Christian, even if we may be reluctant to subscribe to any particular theological system or to give our allegiance to any specific denominational embodiment of the Christian way of existence. Some like me will be prepared to be even more explicit in allegiance to the Christian tradition; but many who cannot accept that engagement are nonetheless ready to admit that they *are* in and of the inheritance which comes to us from our Christian past.

For all of us some real understanding of the development of our Christian background is necessary. We wish to be thoughtful or reflective in whatever use we may make of our inheritance, and to be this, we must see how its insight into the "rightness" of things has come to be, how it has been modified during the centuries, and what it may have to say to us today. But our interest, so far as the present subject is concerned, is not with theological affirmations as such; it centers in the way in which such affirmations have their ethical consequences. How, in fact, has the basic Christian perspective—with its background in the Jewish perspective given us in the Old Testament that is bound up with the New Testament—influenced, perhaps even created, a specific slant or attitude on the "ought"? And to what degree, and in what way, is that attitude or slant a possible one for us today, if our sense of moral responsibility is to be illuminated and our awareness of ethical principles is to be meaningfully related to our inherited tradition, on the one hand, and our contemporary situation, on the other?

It is with such questions that we shall here be concerned, although the fashion in which we attempt to answer them will be more by indirection than by continued and detailed reference.

The members of the primitive tribe or tribes who were the ancestors of the Jewish people are shown to us in the oldest strata of the Old Testament to have been nomadic folk, wandering through the barren regions of the Fertile Crescent and familiar enough with the vagaries of life in that area. They knew of unexpected storms from the desert, of natural disorders such as earthquakes and even volcanic eruptions (Mount Sinai is the significant instance); they knew also of tribal conflict and the quarreling and fighting between those living in settled areas of the country and nomadic interlopers. Whatever may have been their previous religious beliefs—very likely finding deities in such places as springs, "high places," unusual natural phenomena, and the like—they came more and more to find a manifestation of the divine in the occasions that were in their initial impact demonstrations of *power*—power in the realm of nature, power in the relations of humankind, power in extraordinary and unexpected events.

Thus we can see the background for what has come to be called in scholarly circles "primitive Jahwism." Here a dominant tribal deity, Jahweh (or Jehovah), has been identified with release of power. Through the victory of this deity's own tribe over its opponents, Jahweh overcomes deities worshiped by other tribes. Jahweh is made known by violent expressions of strength in natural phenomena. In storm and battle Jahweh is shown to be the strongest of deities, and as such is venerated and given pride of place.

Presently this position of "first" among other deities brings about a tendency toward monotheism, of the sort scholars call "temporary"—at least at this or that time, and in this or that circumstance, this deity is the *only* "god" to be reckoned with. But still Jahweh is disclosed primarily through the catastrophic events in which the enormous power of the deity is shown. The movement, however, does not stop there. The divine is indeed "all-powerful," the one who "shakes the heavens," who "moves the earth," and who acts in terrible and terrifying ways. Yet this deity is also on the side of righteousness. This is the insight that came to the prophets, from the earliest *nebi'im* to the great prophets of Israel once the Jews had settled in Canaan.

The righteousness was initially regarded as required of the Jews among themselves, with insistence on decency and justice among them in their national life. It was also seen in securing for them, whose cause was just and right, victory over the unrighteous and unjust aliens who attacked them and from time to time overcame or oppressed them.

In this connection, tribal mores which doubtless had their origin in necessary habits of social behavior that guaranteed the continued existence of the tribes became identified with what was taken to be the will of Jahweh. Difficult as it is to trace the exact course of development of these "commandments," from whatever prehistoric origins to their enunciation in formal and ordered lists (such as the ten commandments), it is obvious that there was here an interrelationship between the religious convictions of the people and their deepening sense of "oughtness" with respect to human relationships.

As time went on, more profound prophetic understanding came to see that what had begun as tribal customs and practices for the continuation of the people's existence must be interiorized, so that there would be a spirit of obedience to the will of Jahweh, more serious and more penetrating than simple external behavior. Along with this came the awareness that while Jahweh, now taken to be *the* God of the known world, was indeed manifested in exhibitions of power, the basic truth about that power was its concern for the righteousness and justice which was so necessary for a decent and ordered human life. To employ a phrase used by Matthew Arnold with a somewhat different purpose, the power in things was seen to be "the power *that makes for righteousness*." No longer was this sheer power; it was power for social good. And since the primitive God of wars and storms was now also the God of the land and responsible for seedtime and harvest, as well as for summer and winter, this God's concern for righteousness was demonstrated in the settled and orderly processes of life and nature, quite as much as in the extraordinary and catastrophic.

Nor did the development stop at that point, for later prophets, possessed of even more profound insight as they contemplated the course of events and the meaning of human life as they knew it, began to teach that the power that makes for righteousness was at heart characterized by concern, *chesed* (mercy), shown in love for God's people. God therefore expected of the "chosen people" more than mere justice. God also demanded from them a response of obedience, to be shown in their own merciful concern for others, as God had demonstrated the divine merciful concern even when the people had gone astray, disobeyed God's will, and been unfaithful and perverse. Here the teaching of the earlier prophets, an Amos and an Hosea and an Isaiah (not to mention their predecessors, such as Elijah), was carried further by Jeremiah and Second Isaiah. Indeed, Hosea at an earlier time had intimated the love of Jahweh for the chosen people and the requirement that they reflect this love in their own conduct. Now the later prophets made this entirely central in their message.

The only way to true *shalom* (or wholeness and peace) for the people whom Jahweh had chosen and made a covenant with was in a recognition that Jahweh's will was merciful even while it was also righteous. We may say, then, that the development was from power as sheer power, through power seen as exercised for righteousness, to power in righteousness that would establish Jahweh as the loving God who sought and required a response in human caring and concern for others. The "ought" was to reflect that character of love, or *chesed*. Then and only then would a right state of affairs prevail among Jahweh's people.

What is more, the very fact that Israel had been chosen meant that it was Jahweh's purpose to use those chosen servants to bring to all the world this profound understanding of Jahweh's nature and will. The people had been selected, out of all the nations in the earth, to be instrumental in this way, acting for Jahweh in bringing to other nations the truth about this God. Election was not for national pride and aggrandizement but for the service of Jahweh and hence for the benefit of *all* Jahweh's human children, whether they be near or far.

Then came the events associated with the life, teaching, death, and the assurance of the renewed presence of Jesus of

Nazareth. Jesus took over the historic faith of his people. But as Claude Montefiore in his great commentary on the Synoptic Gospels pointed out, there was a notable addition. This was the demonstration in teaching and action that the God of power for righteousness, whose innermost nature was *chesed,* or accepting and caring loving-mercy, went out to initiate the response. God not only accepted those who repented of error, receiving them back with delight and in love, but also, and more significantly, God initiated a search for the erring human creatures. The teaching of Jesus focused on this; his actions expressed this in concrete deeds.

Unquestionably, Jesus' message had to do with the kingly rule of God, which was to be inaugurated in the world and which in God's own activity was shown to humankind ("anticipated eschatology" is the scholarly term for such a view). But the important thing was that "the powers of the age to come" were *already* at work as Jesus himself taught and acted to demonstrate and enact the real quality or character of those powers. And once Jesus had come, had taught, had acted, had died in obedience to that outgoing love of God, and had been seen as risen from the dead because such obedience meant that "he could not be holden of death"—once this had taken place, those who had known him, and others to whom his person and teaching and action were proclaimed, saw that *in him,* in his whole career, from start to finish, that which he had taught and done was itself *embodied.* In Jesus was the love of God going out to God's children; in this human expression of positive initiating care, the divine reality of Love-in-action was not only talked about but concretely and decisively exhibited. Jesus' life was the supreme act of God in the sphere of human existence, not by denying or minimizing other acts of God in the historical realm, but by focusing in an intensive and vivid fashion what God is always up to in the world, how God always acts toward and for God's children, and what God always seeks from them in terms of response.

This means that the "ought" is now seen to be more than the "ought" of righteousness, more even than the "ought" of acceptance and understanding. The imperative is more demanding than that: it is the clear indication that people should go out of themselves, give themselves, concern themselves, and care for others in any and every range of their living. They are to be responsible in *that* way; and this is why some words of Saint John of the Cross, spoken centuries later, can be applied here: "In the evening of our day we shall be judged by our loving." The appraisal of all human action, in every area and aspect of human existence, is in terms of response in love, expressed in human relationships as well as in communion with God.

In the last few pages I have tried to give in summary fashion an account of the way in which the Jewish-Christian religious story has both illuminated and informed awareness of ethical obligation. *The* ethical principle, in its full and adequate expression, is nothing other than love—human loving that both represents and instrumentally serves the divine Love. And I have no doubt that whatever may be amiss in the details of the story as I have summarized it, this *is* the story that the Old and the New Testaments have to tell us. In the next chapter the significance of this central ethical principle will be spelled out more completely; for the present it is enough for us to grasp that such is the deepest insight of the Christian faith with respect to the ethical question. It is just here that what Whitehead liked to call "the brief Galilean vision" has its absolutely central place. That vision brings to completion the earlier insight of the Jewish people; it both crowns and corrects that earlier insight, for the most part by indicating what (as we may put it) God was trying to put across to a segment of the human race during the long course of their troubled history. This is the fulfillment of what went before, for it is the bringing out of the divine intention from the earliest days.

Furthermore, in fulfilling the earlier attempts of the Jews to grasp both the character of God and God's will for humankind, the ethical principle of love-in-action also fulfills the aspirations, insights, and glimpses of God and God's will elsewhere and everywhere. Now that we are coming gradually to know about the non-Jewish and non-Christian religious and ethical traditions, in such civilized lands as India, China, and Japan (to mention but three) and also in less advanced parts of the world, we can also appreciate how these various traditions have succeeded in bringing something of God to their adherents, the nobility of much of their teaching, and the way in which divine activity has nowhere left God without witness. Thus it need no longer be considered part of the Christian claim that only to the biblical story may we attribute divine guidance.

In Professor Macquarrie's *Three Issues in Ethics*, mentioned earlier, there is an eloquent and convincing discussion of this very matter. Dr. Macquarrie shows that Christians not only need not but should not think that to them only (and to their Jewish ancestors in faith, of course) has there been given the ability to grasp the basic ethical issue and to arrive at an answer that is in accordance with what we have styled "the grain of the universe." Theologically, as he insists, that sort of talk is a contradiction of the basic premise of Christian faith—that God is the loving Parent of *all* God's children, wherever they may live and in whatever period of history. Beyond that, to talk in this manner is to convict oneself of ignorance and prejudice by failing to see that there are indeed intimations and hints, indeed many clear expressions, of the same awareness of ethical obligation. What is more, this obligation is plainly a development toward what we should style an ethic of love. The fact that in the history of the Jews, in the climaxing of that history in Jesus Christ, and in the continuing life of the Christian community a decisive disclosure of divine intention has been given does not in any way invalidate what in other times and places has been learned about that intention. We may legitimately talk of our experience and conviction that there is a focal disclosure; we have no right to dismiss as irrelevant, much less as false, the ethical insights of other people in other lands and at other times, and all this thanks to the religious beliefs that such people sincerely held.

In recent years renewed attention has been given to the ethical material found in the New Testament; this ethical material has been studied with deeper grasp of its locus in a basically religious context. No longer is it assumed that we can excise the faith which the New Testament both reflects and states and concern ourselves only with the ethics of the New Testament. Jesus was not primarily an ethical teacher; he was one who announced and embodied the divine kingdom or rule in the world. Paul was not an itinerant teacher of sound ethical principles; he was an evangelist for Jesus Christ as God's signal act in human history. Hence, in contemporary study of New Testament ethics the point of origin is taken to be the religious stance of those who put in writing the material we possess—and, a fortiori, the religious stance of those for whom they wrote, as well as those who provided them with the traditions and memories that they have put into writing.

J.L. Houlden, formerly Principal of Cuddesden Theological College, has published an admirable if brief discussion of this subject. In that work, *Ethics and the New Testament* (New York: Penguin Books, 1973), Houlden has demonstrated both the variety and the unity of the New Testament's recording of primitive Christian ethical understanding. He has shown how absurd it is to attempt to reduce the material to a single pattern; at the same time, he has shown that there is one central theme which runs through all the different emphases of ethical teaching, the theme of love. The variations are to be explained by several factors: the differences in background of the writers or those for whom they wrote, the ways in which now this person and now that person interpreted the earlier Jewish ethical tradition, the need to relate the central theme to the circumstances in which early Christians found themselves, the problems that were being faced and the resources available for facing them.

Thus we cannot steamroller the diversity and make everything neat and tidy. Yet on the other hand we can discern in that very diversity a basic insistence on the ethical obligation to reflect in human life the divine Charity or Love that is disclosed in the event we name when we say "Jesus Christ."

One aspect of this process of development has been the way in which the older Jewish Law (the Torah), taken as God's revealed will and God's requirements of humankind, has been related to the central theme of love. And it is just here that we can profit by studies such as that by Houlden. Altogether too often in discussions of the course of Christian history and the relation of the Law and the Summary of the Law, it has been suggested that in thus "summarizing" Jesus and the primitive Christian community validated the entire older ethical position even while they also brought out its hidden meaning. In one sense, of course, this is correct, if by validation we mean simply recognizing or acknowledging the value of what was said by the ancestors of Israel as they came to grasp more profoundly the divine requirement. But it is not correct if this validation is taken to be nothing other than an insistence that the position of the "older dispensation" is to be taken over as a whole by those who belong to the "newer dispensation." Even with respect to the ten commandments this cannot be so. Certainly from that listing of God's supposed demands upon the chosen people we can discern the ways in which a primitive people were being educated or trained in ethical insight. Furthermore, even in our own day, not to speak of the days of the primitive Christian community, the ten commandments can be said to hint at the social pattern of behavior that (when suitably adapted to another time and place) will bring out a state of affairs which promotes the best fulfillment of personhood in society. To say this, however, is not to affirm that the Christian ethical stance is identical with that enunciated in the ten commandments as they stand. In any event, the requirements there stated do not stand alone; they are in the context of a prior faith—which is why it is Jewish practice to put the *Shema* (Hear O Israel, the Lord our God is one God . . .") first, before the commandments are repeated. And they cannot readily be adapted to a culture that does not simply repeat the situation of the period in which they were given and to which obviously they were intended to apply.

The real trouble with taking the ten commandments or any other legal version of ethical principle as if they were given once and for all is that the relationship between God and God's children is not a legal one but a familial one. When ethical wrongdoing is regarded as a violation of legal enactment, even *divine* legal enactment, the whole situation is misrepresented. In the terms we have used earlier, the "ought" in human existence is related in no legalistic or forensic fashion to "the way things go in the world." It is a *reflection* of that way, not an established set of regulations that are to be obeyed as if we lived in a world where things continued always in one fixed position. The words of James Russell Lowell, quoted earlier, apply here with enormous force: "*New* occasions teach *new* duties. . . ." And "occasions" are *always* new, with each succeeding generation and even (although this must be said with proper caution) with each different person in his or her own concrete situation and circumstances.

Thomas Aquinas, with his usual penetration, saw the real point when (with all his respect for and acceptance of the religio-ethical tradition he inherited) he insisted that "the new law in our hearts" is nothing other than the love disclosed and imparted in Jesus Christ and by the Holy Spirit—who, as a New Testament text reminds us, "takes of the things of Christ and declares them unto us." This insight establishes the freedom of the Christian, as Luther so frequently was to insist. What is more, it also establishes the freedom of any person, anywhere and at any time, to see his or her own ethical obligation in its concrete relation to the particular time and place (always bearing in mind the nearly universal awareness that this obligation is centrally given in the commandment, if we may call it such, "Love one another") and in consequence to try to act always in love.

The content of that love must be spelled out in more detail, of course. Suffice it to say at this point that is it not sentimentality, nor easy tolerance of anything and everything, nor soft-hearted goodwill, nor merely an emotional affair. On the contrary, it is exacting, demanding, and hard. It is precisely here that the figure of Jesus Christ is so important. The love that is our ethical obligation, our "ought," is *that* sort of love. It is a stern love that demands and expects human fulfillment in relationship with others; but it is also a love that suffers with those others, bearing their burdens, entering into their sorrow, and sharing their anguish. This is no easy business; it takes all there is of a person and is never satisfied until and unless that person is giving that all. In other words, it is like the love which is of God and which is God, the love that is the very grain of the universe, the "rightness" in things, and "the way the world goes." Anybody who could think that such an ethical principle is less demanding than legalistic obedience to supposedly divine fiat is clearly either stupid or frivolous.

3

Love and Ethical Principle

3

Love and Ethical Principle

Love is the central ethical principle, nothing more and nothing less. That is the conclusion of our discussion up to this point. As far as the Jewish-Christian story is concerned, it is the culmination of a long and painful process of discovery, as people of great insight attempted to make sense of their experience, of the history of their nation, and of what they believed to be the activity of God in the created world. From power, through righteousness and loving-mercy, to outgoing and positive concern and the adamant love that reflects the divine character: that is the way it went.

Or, to put it another way, it is the account of a movement in which we proceed from obedience to laws that have been laid down, as it is supposed once for all in a divine revelation, to a life with one's brothers and sisters in mutual care, sympathy, courage, helpfulness, and understanding. Love is the fulfilling of the Law, as Paul wrote (Romans 13:8). What the Torah was getting at in legalistic fashion was love of the sort disclosed in Christ effectively demonstrated in the life of One Person, now to be shared by all people.

But if this is the case, in whichever manner we state it, we still have to reckon with some inescapable questions. We have to ask about the relationship between such love and the righteousness—call it justice, if you wish—that "alone exalteth a people," the kind of dealing in which each person will receive his or her due and each will also give his or her neighbor that due. And we also must ask about the place of *rules*, for can we properly speak of ethical obligation without introducing the notion of rules to be followed in the implementing of love? These are among the problems we shall be concerned with in this chapter.

We must do this for several reasons, the most important of which is the frequently repeated objection that an ethical principle like love-in-action is altogether too ideal, too abstract, too lacking in content. It is easy to say that we are to love our brothers and sisters as God has loved us, yet it is difficult if not impossible to put this into practice. When we do, surely we are obliged to talk about the rules that ought to be followed in specific instances, as we are also obliged to reckon with the possibility that in pursuing the so-called ideal of love we may very well do an injustice to our brothers and sisters, failing to recognize that they too "ought" to have their rights and "ought" to be given their just place in society.

If there are no rules to be followed in the moral life of humankind, and if the only possible appeal is to the ethical principle of love, is there not also a real danger of antinomianism? In the early days of Christian faith, even in the primitive communities to which Paul addressed his letters, such antinomianism was indeed a threat. Some Christians, rejoicing in their newfound freedom from the Jewish Law or in the liberty to which as Gentile converts they had been admitted, felt that there could be no restraints upon their behavior. After all, "the freedom wherewith Christ has made us free" (cf. Galatians 5:1) might well seem to them freedom to do what they wished, when and how they wished it. Total lawlessness—antinomianism—could be a consequence. To this problem Paul gave full attention, insisting that the emphasis on love as the central ethical principle did not and could not imply that there were no secondary principles. He urged that the Law was no longer binding on Christians but that it provided what we today might wish to call guidelines as to the ways in which the central ethical principle of love could be put to work.

I believe it is necessary to see that Paul was quite correct in his worry about and attack on such antinomianism. But it may also be possible for us to put his case in another and perhaps more satisfactory way; and we shall proceed now to consider this, before going on to the question of justice in relationship to love.

Let me begin by urging that the very centrality of the principle of love of necessity *rules out* certain kinds of behavior, whether this be in thought or word or deed. It will be noticed that this is a *negative* statement—ruling *out*. The notion that ethical rules or codes are primarily permanent positive directives, giving in detail information as to how one should act in given circumstances, is difficult because the circumstances in which people find themselves are bound to change and a rule or code that would be suitable in one situation might very well not be suitable in another. Of course, there is a sense in which what I above called guidelines do have a positive aspect. That is, they indicate the direction in which "right" behavior should move, even if they do not provide explicit directives in this or that instance. Here once more we need to stress the processive nature of the human enterprise and the creation as a whole. It might be quite proper to talk about explicit regulations governing conduct in any and every circumstance, were it also the case that human nature is fixed and that the world itself is also a fixed order. In that way, circumstances would indeed change in some respects, but essentially there would be a sufficiently permanent state of affairs to make prescription possible. In a processive world, however, with human existence as movement toward fulfillment of potentiality, there is inevitably a certain relativity about everything. Talk of absolutes in such a world is possible only when these are sufficiently general, sufficiently patient of varied implementation, to avoid a suggestion of a static situation.

But I have said that there can be what I have styled a

"ruling *out.*" In my book *Love and Control in Sexuality* (New York: The Pilgrim Press, 1974) I have suggested how this can be seen in one important aspect of human existence. If love is the central ethical principle that must be applied to any and every area, it is nowhere more obviously the norm than in matters of sexual conduct. We can readily see that love requires, by its own perspective, the avoidance of any sort of behavior that imperils love itself. In the book just mentioned I argued that love is contradicted by self-centered, cruel, depersonalizing, irresponsible, and inordinate acts. It is not so much a question of externally imposed rules or regulations, as if a voice had spoken from on high telling children exactly what they were or were not to do. The question is rather what love itself, as the governing "ought" in human life, necessarily entails—in this instance, in matters of sexual conduct.

Furthermore, the indication that the direction to be taken in the sexual expression of love precludes (rules out) self-centeredness, cruelty, depersonalization, irresponsibility, and inordination (or such emphasis upon physical sex that its wider setting in shared life is forgotten or rejected) is not merely a business of human decision. It is indeed such a matter, but it is in accordance with what we have consistently spoken of as the way the world goes. The cosmos is set up in such a fashion that its dynamic is marked by exactly the opposite of the self-centeredness, etc., which damage or destroy love in sexual life. It is a world where there is societal relationship, where each occasion is so much in contact with other occasions that mutuality is required, where every act has consequences that affect other people, and where there is a proportion in things.

Alfred North Whitehead spoke about ethical intent as involving intensity, vividness, and harmony. This admirable summary may be applied to our present problem. Intensity or the full assent with heart and soul and mind to the enterprise being undertaken; vividness or a profound awareness of the demands of a love that itself is movingly and tellingly in God and in what God does in the world; and harmony or the ordering of affairs in such a way that no single aspect or area or element pretends to claim that it and it alone is worthy of attention: in these three we have a way of looking at love as central ethical principle. And in the application of that principle to our daily life, with all its problems and possibilities, the same threefold pattern is appropriate. The "ought" in human existence—the "ought" which tells us that we are to live in love toward and with other human beings—is to be followed with intensity; we are to do the works of love with all our energy and with total personal commitment or engagement. It is to be followed in an awareness of its "importance" (to use a Whiteheadian term), precisely because it *matters* and has been shown to matter by the disclosure that the chief causative and receptive agency (God) is itself just such Love-in-action. And it is to be followed in a fashion that promotes harmonization or concord among people, so that each lives for others and all concern themselves with the proper fulfillment of each.

I have just used the words "total personal commitment or engagement." These words recall that earlier we have seen how significant in ethical life is the giving of self to the human enterprise—and to particular responsibilities which appear in that enterprise, too. We are indebted to contemporary existentialist writers for a renewed stress on commitment or engagement. Following the lead given by the great Danish thinker Søren Kierkegaard (who himself is in a tradition including names like Augustine, Martin Luther, and Pascal), existentialism has pointed out that human ethical existence is no bare and abstract speculative matter but is marked by the making of insignificant decisions. These decisions are not the result of a cool, objective consideration, nor are they purely rational choices that are made in isolation from the exigencies of daily life. On the contrary, they are cases of "subjective pathos," based on deep feelings and compelling personal interest. *I* am at the center of the business of decision, and whatever I decide involves *all of me*. In a properly ethical choice, I necessarily stake my very existence on and give myself unreservedly to that for which I have decided.

Admittedly, this may seem a somewhat overheated portrayal of what actually takes place in many of our acts of choice. We do not in fact live in a never-ending series of ethical crises, such as this analysis might suggest. Nonetheless, the existentialists are correct in their view that commitment, personal intensity, full human assent, and the willingness to act with wholehearted dedication are the very heart of human ethical life, however it may be with this or that specific decision. Perhaps we may say that it is the "big" choices, the decisions of decisive importance, which vividly demonstrate the existentialists' point, while the "smaller," less decisive, choices are related to these, either as further applications of the big and decisive one (or ones) or as falling within the line or direction that the latter have laid down. In any event, Whitehead's insistence on intensity and the existentialist stress on commitment indicate that if human ethical life is to be truly human *and* truly ethical, it cannot be a matter of indifference, of tepid acceptance of conditions or circumstances, or of simple conventionality (doing what the Joneses do). There is all the difference in the world between acquiescence in the public and its ways (to put it in Kierkegaardian language) and a genuinely and fully responsible ethical life.

Such decisions entail that people possess at least a minimum of freedom. Obviously there are limits to this, since (to take an obvious example) those who happen to live in California are hardly in the position to choose what would be possible only if they had their residence in the Sahara Desert and vice versa. Further, the degree of freedom is to a considerable extent determined by the past that one has inherited as well as by the past decisions one has made. In other ways, too, the limit of free choice is apparent to us. Nonetheless, as Bishop Joseph Butler pointed out long ago in *The Analogy of Religion* (London: Knapton, 1736), we do in fact act as if we had some significant freedom of choice and hence of decision; all experience, he said, points to such a situation, and theories that deny what we know full well are artificial and abstract. The very language we use is meaningless unless we are thus free.

Now I suggest that this experienced sense of freedom is a pointer toward a more pervasive fact about the world at large. Although the lower levels of that world plainly do not have the consciousness of freedom we possess, they *do* opt (in their own appropriate manner) for *this* rather than for *that*. Indeed, as has often been pointed out, the word decision is derived from the Latin *decidere*, which means "to cut off." When a quantum of energy "jumps" in one direction it cuts off the possibility of jumping in another. Straight through the cosmos, we may contend, there is this fact of decision in the root meaning of the word; hence there is an element of chance in the world as a whole. It is not all laid on the line, predetermined in a fashion that would suggest the sort of control which allows no room for options of any kind, conscious or unconscious. It will be noticed, I trust, that this is not an argument for vitalism in, say, the realm of biological phenomena, with an "entelechy" or spirit *in addition to* the observable physical or physiological details. It is simply the recognition that at any level of integration there is some uncertainty about which way this or that particular entity will move. Doubtless the chanciness, as it may be styled, is held under control in an ultimate sense; one of the chief arguments for a divine agency in the cosmos is that the sort of chance we have argued for does not end in sheer chaos or anarchy. There is a way in which things are kept in balance and that is why we can speak meaningfully, both from introspection and from observation, of a *cosmos*.

Once more, then, we see that the ethical sense in human beings, assured that they can and do act with a genuine freedom (however limited in extent), is in accordance with a principle that runs through the whole creation. Humankind's awareness that there is freedom to choose for or against genuine self-fulfillment in relationship with others is not a purely subjective and illusory experience; it is one with the grain of the universe, to repeat again the phrase used earlier.

In Hazel Barnes's interesting study *An Existentialist Ethics* (New York: Knopf, 1967), one of her main arguments against a theistic interpretation of human existence is that theism propounds a view of deity in which absolute control is an integral element. This view, she rightly urges, denies the plain empirical fact of human consciousness of decisions in such freedom as make a difference in how things will go in the future. A person becomes nothing more than an automaton who must do what the absolute will of the deity imposes. We have here another illustration of the damage that has been done by the classical theism against which Prof. Charles Hartshorne and other process philosophers have battled. When the religious conviction of divine perfection is translated into the metaphysical assertion of absoluteness of *that* kind, a grave mistake in logic and theology is being made. And when with this absoluteness there is combined the notion that God is self-contained, unable to enjoy any experience (to use a perhaps inappropriate word) of "becoming," and entirely unaffected by what goes on in the world through creaturely decisions, our difficulty is compounded. That conception of God has always failed to give due place to humankind's ethical possibility, to a person's capacity to say yes or no in any significant sense that implies genuine consequences, and to the responsibility that a person feels to do what "ought" to be done if that person is to actualize his or her possibilities and to share fully with brothers and sisters in the social existence without which a person has no worth or value. But another conception of God is entirely possible; and "neoclassical theism" or "dipolar theism," which Hartshorne has defended so ably, carries with it no such denial of human ethical integrity.

Before we proceed to a consideration of love and justice, it may be useful to look further at the relationship of such codified laws as the ten commandments to the central ethical principle of love. This is all the more necessary because of the persistent feeling that only when such codes are maintained can there be any hope of genuine morality among humankind in society. Without an abiding ethical code that is accepted as an explicit disclosure of the divine will, it is said, human beings are likely to run amok. People, being what they are, must be controlled; and such control can only come from outside and beyond the human situation.

Probably no honest person will deny that there *is* a strong tendency in people to act without regard for ethical consequences—or, to put it in a better way, to act for their own ends with little concern for others. This is the sort of situation that is in view when traditional religious language speaks about "original sin" and "concupiscence." The former points to a situation in which human insight is distorted and human energy is enfeebled; the latter has to do with a persistent drive in people to get their own way without bothering about consequences. At the same time, we must not forget that there is also in the human heart a capacity to respond to invitations to goodness, an admiration for decency and generosity, and a yearning for open and helpful relations with others. Paul himself saw this and spoke of the strange duality of the situation, for people see what they "ought" to do but find they do not want to do it, while at the same time they can see what they "ought" not to do yet discover themselves actually doing it. "I see the better; I follow the worse"—so said the old Latin writer. But also I *do* try to follow the better, time and again; and I find that I cannot do it, hard as I may strive.

This is true enough, but it is difficult to see how a codified and supposedly permanent ethical law can do other than make the situation worse. For when I am told by an external authority that I must do this, there is the corollary implicit in that statement that if I do *not* do what I am told I shall be punished. In other words, a reward-and-punishment motif is inevitably introduced. This can bring about either servile obedience or determination to disobey. In either case, there is no ethical response. If there is an "ought" integral to human existence, it has to be self-authenticating; it must also be self-validating, in the sense that it must plainly carry with it an awareness of the unhappy consequences for human growth, if one fails to respond, or the desirable ones, if response is made positively. "Virtue is its own reward," says the old saw, and I believe that human experience demonstrates the truth of the saying. It was Dean Inge of St. Paul's in London who once remarked, if I remember rightly, that an ethic based upon the reward-punishment motif resembles nothing so much as the method by which one invests money in shares or bonds. And he quoted the words of a hymn

Whatever, Lord, I give to thee
Ten thousandfold repaid will be

as a perfect illustration of what is wrong with the notion that I am to do good because it is suitably rewarded. Whatever else may be said, it is hardly a very high ethical principle.

But as I suggested earlier, we can recognize that the ten commandments, and similar codifications of ethical obligation, do have a genuine, indeed a high, value. They tell us how our remote ancestors, as well as many in times nearer to our own, were able to grow in moral discernment and to come to understand that antisocial behavior (illicit sexual acts, disregard of others, covetousness and greed, hatred and murder) damages the stability and integrity of human life, both personal and social. Some years ago Bernard Meland suggested that we might well attempt to write our own commandments; perhaps that was an extreme view, but what Dr. Meland was getting at was sound enough. *As they stand*, in their literal sense, the negatives of the ten commandments do not belong to our culture; they must always be reinterpreted. Indeed, that is what those who are their vigorous defenders constantly do. It is also apparent that we require a much more positive statement of whatever rules may be helpful to us—not what we must *avoid* doing but what we must set out *to do*. And the whole point of Jesus' Summary of the Law—his bringing out what was its divine purpose, ethically speaking—is to be found precisely in that positive quality. The "ought" in human existence is the necessity to live in love, not only the necessity (under pain of punishment) of avoiding certain specific acts.

Probably it was Thomas Aquinas' awareness of this sort of difficulty in codified legalistic ethics that brought him to rely much more on the natural law, the ethical awareness that is given in human nature as the creation of God; "the evil is to be avoided," he says, but he also says that "the good is to be done." As we have seen, he found "the new law" to be charity or love in our hearts. When he came to spell out what this implied in concrete practice, he naturally talked in terms of his thirteenth-century milieu; he could not have done otherwise. But he had the order of things right, and we must respect him for it.

We may now turn to the business of justice as it is related to the central ethical principle of love. First of all, we need to discard the idea that there is a necessary conflict between the two. Of course, if we think of love as sentimentality or emotion, and nothing more, there appears to be a real problem. Justice has to do with our seeing that each person gets what is his or her human right and it requires that each person perform his or her human duty. It is altogether too easy to say that we love our neighbor, in an emotional fashion, without bothering much about our neighbor's rights and without concerning ourselves with our duty toward our neighbor. But this is not love in the profound sense in which we have been discussing it.

In another book, *Love Looks Deep* (Oxford: Mowbrays, 1969), I attempted to present what I there styled a phenomenology of love—that is, what love really is as it presents itself to us in our deepest human experience. I urged that love includes the following ingredients: commitment or engagement for the the good of the other or others, mutuality or openness to others and willingness to give-and-take, faithfulness to those whom we say we love, hopefulness or expectation that from our relationship better and more enriching life will follow, and an urgent desire for as intimate and complete a communion between persons as is possible for both parties. My primary interest in working out that description was in the matter of personal relationships. But I believe that these five ingredients are equally relevant in social affairs, among the various groups and classes in a nation and among the nations of the earth. If this is the case, then we can say that justice will be the means by which such love will be given its adequate social expression.

Unless and until these groups can see each other in terms of commitment, mutual trust, faithfulness to undertakings agreed upon, hopefulness that such undertakings will be fruitful in better life for all concerned, and a genuine desire for a common life, there can be no hope for the world. The ethical responsibility of each group is to be ready to think and act along these lines. That means working out the concrete measures that will ensure just such cooperation. Otherwise the affairs of humankind in society, and of nations with one another, will be exactly what Augustine said they were: a sort of legalized brigandage—*latrocinia*. Of course in social life of all sorts there must be some system by which evil individuals or groups can be restrained, lest they do enormous damage to the body politic and to the national and international order. But the most important question is that of motivation. And almost any reflective person knows perfectly well that unless there is an abundant measure of what we usually call goodwill, no amount of restraint is going to produce a happy state of affairs.

One illustration occurs to me. We know that in respect to racial relationships, whether in the United States or in the increasingly problematic situation in Great Britain, it is incumbent upon us to see to it that all people and all groups—be they black or white, red or yellow—shall have their proper rights. If nothing else had taught us this necessity, it would be plain enough from the inevitable revolt of those who have been or are being oppressed. They demand their full human rights. That is justice in the ordinary sense of the word. But there is a deeper justice, one that is profoundly related to the central ethical principl of love. I can work with might and main to guarantee rights by legal enactment; and I must do so—that is what love-in-action requires of me. At the same time, I must care for persons of another race, setting myself to be brother or sister to them in every way open for me and creating new ways when the old ones seem to fail. Each of those brothers or sisters is a person, moving toward fulfillment of his or her potentiality or being prevented from that fulfillment by particular circumstances. Each is my equal *as* a human being, whatever differences there may be in talent or education or anything else that makes him or her *that* person and not some other person. Here again love-in-action provides the imperative to concern and to caring.

The purpose of the movement for social justice, economic opportunity, communal cooperation, international peace, and the like is the provision of such conditions as shall be inspired by love in the former manner, so that love in the latter manner may more completely be experienced among us all. Otherwise we are talking about cold justice, and that in effect is only prudential and not ethical. Few of us, surely, would think that *fear* is an ethical principle.

4

Love as the Absolute

4

Love as the Absolute

Love is indeed the central ethical principle, but not because it simply happens to be subjectively a "good thing." People have come to recognize this, confident that love in human relations is in accordance with the deepest reality in things—with how the world really goes, as we have put it. The chief causative agency in the world is not power but love; that has been part of our argument, based as it is on the conviction that in a world in process, where things are always "coming to be," what Whitehead called persuasion is more basic than coercion. Process and love: these two are integral to the world and to human experience.

Obviously there is much that is wrong. There is evil in the world, and a full account would have much to say about this. Disorder, distortion, decisions that prevent realization of good, cruelty among human beings and in nature—all certainly exist and must be reckoned with. However, for our present purpose—which is to determine, so far as we can, how best to understand the meaning of the "ought" in human experience—we need not spend our time in considering how such evil in its various forms may best be envisaged, how it arises, and what its significance is in the total picture. In my book *Goodness Distorted* (Oxford: Mowbrays, 1970), I have discussed evil in the broader sense, and in the more recent *Cosmic Love and*

Human Wrong (New York: Paulist Press, 1978) I have attempted a restatement of the meaning of "sin," or willful wrong human conduct (in thought, as well as in word and act), in the light of a process conception of the universe. I refer any interested reader to those books for an account of how at least one modern Christian theologician would state the case.

Here I simply assert once more that the conclusion of our argument up until this point is that we may reasonably hold love to be the central ethical principle. But to say this suggests another question. Is there nothing absolute in ethical life? After all, it may be said that love itself is a very relative matter. Furthermore, have we not said again and again that circumstances alter cases? And does not that imply that there is nothing to which we may appeal unfailingly, nothing which may be given the status of absolute and unchanging authority? In this chapter we shall look at this question of absolute and relative in ethical discussion, recognizing that for many people it is the most important aspect of the whole business.

In dealing with this matter we must first of all stress once again the view of the world as a changing or developing process. We repeat that process does not equal progress and that nobody in his senses would claim that "every day, in every way, we're getting better and better." Yet there is process or development. And this is marked both by continuity and by the appearance of the genuinely new. Thus there are persisting patterns or ways of organization, on the one hand, while on the other there are novel emergences that (once they have taken place) make a difference in future patterning or organization. To use the simplest example, hydrogen and oxygen continue, but the kind of organization or patterning that chemists describe as H_2O is a novel emergent, namely, water. Water is still composed of the elements of hydrogen and oxygen, but the way in which they are together as water has made and continues to make a difference.

Now in the history of the cosmos, if we may use this way

of putting it (and appropriately so, since today we know that nature is not simply repetitive or circular, but is getting somewhere and hence has a linear or historical character), humankind has made its appearance. Just how, where, and when are matters for experts in the particular scientific disciplines to consider; but the fact is plain enough—and *we* are that fact. Having emerged at some point in the process, humankind is continuous with what has gone before and what is going on now around it, but it is also different. Humankind is made up of *human beings*. Human beings are not simply sophisticated animals (although they share much with the animal world), nor are they angels, simply "spiritual" in nature. Human beings are both bodily and spiritual.

Prof. Harold K. Schilling has written admirably about the emergence of humankind in a recent book devoted to what he styles "the new consciousness" found in both scientific and religious disciplines:

> When [the human being] arrived, evolutionary activity took on a new character. His extraordinary powers enabled him quickly to bring forth a great variety of utterly new realities: tools and processes, abstractions and symbols, languages and logics, rational analyses and syntheses, measurement and experimentation, and many others equally unprecedented. In this way social rather than biological evolution came to dominate change. The arts and literatures emerged, and the religions, and philosophies, laws, the sciences and technologies—and thus man's cultures and civilizations, with new orders of good and evil, beauty and ugliness, truth and deception. (*The New Consciousness in Science and Religion* [New York: The Pilgrim Press, 1973], p. 148.)

Nor is that all that can be said. Dr. Schilling goes on to tell us:

> There came to this new being the capacity for self-analysis which was quite unprecedented. He learned to investigate

> himself, as well as his world, with both critical objectivity and discriminating introspection—and *in depth*. He discovered that his "self," his so-called "nature," and his tremendously varied potentialities are not "possessions" or innate attributes of his own but in large part the gift-consequences of his relationships with other entities and processes and with nature as a whole. Through his knowledge and understanding he has achieved a remarkable degree of self-determination. To a large extent he is now in a position to be both the architect and builder of his own future, which could certainly not be said about any of his evolutionary forebears. (Ibid., pp. 148–49.)

This is said well, and we must give it our fullest attention when we consider who a human being is—who this being is, to whom the sense of "ought" or ethical responsibility, is integral. That is to say, precisely because human beings have emerged as the sort of creatures that Dr. Schilling has described, they are aware of such a "degree of self-determination," with the freedom of decision that accompanies such a possibility, that they can be adequately understood only as creatures who meaningfully can say "ought." Indeed, of human beings alone (so far as we can see) could it be meaningful to say that they can *become* human beings, through their own decisions and with the employment of the materials that are presented to them in and from the world, including of course their own earlier specifically human patterning. G.K. Chesterton once remarked that one would not tell a crocodile, "Be a crocodile," since the crocodile is what it is to the limit of its possibility. But to a person, Chesterton said, it *is* possible to say, "Be a human being, that is, strive to become what potentially you are." This is self-determination and this is what makes human beings unique, since they only (as Dr. Schilling has told us) are "in a position to be both the architect and builder of [their] own future."

Nor is Dr. Schilling alone in speaking in this way. From a Christian theological stance, and writing about ethical issues in our own day, the German thinker Jürgen Moltmann has said this:

> The "struggle for existence" is connected with the elementary interest of man in his personal liberation from dependence of nature in his surroundings and in his own body. It is the other side of his will for power over nature and himself. Since man has become independent of nature, and to the extent to which he becomes powerful over nature, he becomes a "human being," i.e., a person capable of action. Today it is becoming more and more possible for him to determine not only his spiritual and private, but also his physical and social existence. Liberation and power are, however, only of interest so long as one does not have them. The more man gains them, the more questionable becomes the human being who has to plan and live. "What are human beings here for?" ("Hope and the Biomedical Future of Man," in Ewert H. Cousins, ed., *Hope and the Future of Man* [Philadelphia: Fortress Press, 1972], pp. 93–94.)

So far, then, for Moltmann's portrayal of what has brought humankind where it is. He goes on, however, to tell us that he agrees with Julian Huxley's insistence that "after the 'struggle for existence,' the 'striving for fulfilment,' i.e., for the fulfillment of human possibilities, will come more and more into the foreground." This means, for Huxley, that "in the course of scientific and technical progress, man—seen positively—can enter into a previously unsuspected realization" of human destiny. It would be possible to interpret this as suggesting that humankind is to be entirely independent of anything or anyone suprahuman; but it might also be possible, and this Professor Moltmann believes, to see that "the destiny of mankind in the image of the creative God" is in no way contradictory to the fullest freedom and responsibility which the human race can claim for itself (ibid., p. 94).

I have given these extended quotations because they show two important aspects of the ethical situation. First, they help us to see that while humankind is continuous with the natural order from which it has emerged and in which it exists, at the same time there is something distinctive about it. And second, they indicate that this distinctive human quality is found in the capacity for self-determination, so that human choices are significant not only for proper fulfillment of men and women as human beings but also for the ongoing of the creative process itself. In words made familiar to us by so many contemporary writers, humankind has "come of age" (Dietrich Bonhoeffer, the German Christian martyr to the Nazis, first phrased it that way) and hence men and women can only rightly see themselves as responsible creatures who can no longer turn, as once they were prone to do, to a deus ex machina to rescue them from the unhappy consequences of their own acts. Yet this does not mean, nor for Schilling and Moltmann does it suggest, the kind of independence that rejects altogether the reality of God, of God's purpose for the world, and of the personalized use which God makes of human agents to work toward the accomplishment of that purpose. Men and women are in the image of the creative God, and their proper fulfillment, in terms of human destiny, is at the same time their proper cooperation with the cosmic thrust. God is no deus ex machina but is unfailingly present in and active through the world. Charles Hartshorne likes to say that the divine intention is that God's creatures shall make themselves. That is their freedom and that is their responsibility.

If this be true, then the "ought" in human experience is most deeply related to the creative God's purpose. On the other hand, precisely because that "ought" is not spelled out in detail, there is an inescapable relativity in ethical decision. Hence we are brought back once more to our question: Is everything relative or is there something that is absolute because it is always and everywhere the case? We return to the view that the central ethical principle is love, working itself out in concrete situations. This is the absolute in ethics, and everything else is to some degree and in some fashion relative.

Relativity is an ambiguous word, however, and we should be quite clear about its meaning in this context. I am not for a moment suggesting that it should imply that anything goes and that there are no right and sound lines of advance. Far from such a state of affairs, I should urge that to think (and act) on that assumption would be to give up the ethical altogether. Nor in fact would this be genuine relativity, as I intend it; it would be sheer anarchy. On the other hand, there is a relativity that consists in the frank acceptance of the truth, so often asserted in these pages, that "circumstances alter cases" and that "new occasions teach new duties." In that case there could very well be something abiding and permanent in terms of the human "ought," but its very permanence would require that it be adapted to the varying conditions in which people find themselves. We should be prepared to acknowledge certain lines of advance that are right for the human race and for individuals, yet there would be sufficient openness to allow adjustment to differing situations.

Here again we may claim that such a position is in accordance with the basic dynamic in the world. On the theistic view adopted in this book, we have seen that there is a chief causative agency in the world whose nature and name is Love. We have spoken of this agency as actively at work luring that world toward its proper fulfillment of possibility. This fulfillment is the realization of a shared good, in which all participate and to which all contribute. Yet at different times in human history, to take the level that matters most to us, as well as at different places in that long story, the general purpose of shared good may be better appropriated. These are by no means always identical instances. Here one sort of activity is required; there, another. To put this in simple religious language, the divine will remains constant; it is always for the greatest attainable good in any and every situation. Yet God works in those particular situations in the particular ways that are appropriate to them. The history of human ethical development demonstrates this. In primitive times the only available way to disclose cosmic good was through showing first that divine power is truly at work in the world. But later the way was by the manifestation of that power as concerned above all for personal and social righteousness. Then came the time when loving-mercy, forgiveness, and acceptance were shown to be the essential divine nature. In each instance God adapted to that which humankind was able to understand and accept.

So also for our own human ethical growth. To move from barbaric existence toward ordered social life; then to move on to deepening recognition of the conditions that make social life enriching for all who are part of it; and so finally to come to see that "it's love and love alone" (as the old song has it) which men and women really want and which alone can bring them genuine fulfillment—here is the story of the development of ethical insight. It would be a mistake to denounce those who have preceded us for doing, saying, and behaving as they were convinced was right. It would also be a mistake for us to try to return to some earlier stage in the development. At one and the same time we can learn from the past, and yet be loyal to our own present insight.

The relativity about which I am speaking, therefore, is not an anarchic state of affairs; it is the perception that there must be adaptation of the central ethical principle to the given situation and more particularly an adaptation that will allow for further advance, for deepening insight, and for more adequate expression of the principle itself. I urge that love is absolute; but I also say that we know it, and in our finite human natures can know it only, in and through the relativities of our existence, wherever we may be. This is not to argue that, in being absolute, love is a remote and idealistic notion; on the contrary, it is to see that love is immediate and concrete in its challenge and in its capacity to enable action. That is very different from an entirely content-less ideal, on the one hand, and from simple acquiescence in the obvious immediacies we know, on the other. Ethical life is a continuing interplay between love with its absolute demand *and* the daily responsibilities that we must meet. It is both a judgment upon us and an imperative for us. It makes impossible contentment with things as they are and it impels us to bend our every effort to make things more and more conformable to love, and loving relationships, as the proper norm for human existence.

Now, under such circumstances we are bound to make mistakes, we are bound to fail. If this were a world where everything is neatly arranged, it might conceivably be possible (once we had the right perspective) to go along in an entirely perfect fashion, so far as human finitude would permit. But our world is not like that at all. It is the sort of world that we have been describing, with an element of chance running through it but with sufficient control to prevent such uncertainty from reduction to chaos; it is a world where creaturely decisions count and have their consequences; it is a world where nothing creaturely is absolutely fixed. The *only* absolute is the love that is God—or God who is Love. And in such a world, error is bound to occur, wrong judgments are certain to be made, and mistakes will surely happen. The world is more like a great adventure than it is like a settled scheme with every detail precisely set forth.

In our ethical lives, therefore, we are obliged to reckon with failures; we are also forced to take thought about what we are to do. But it is at the same time a world in which living has zest and joy, with an appeal to our imagination quite as much as a demand for our thoughtful consideration. We could even say that it is a world where there are bound to be calculated risks—risks because everything is not laid on the line, and *calculated* risks because we have to think about what is our obligation, what are our responsibilities, and how best we may do that which we "ought" to do as human beings.

For those who hold the Christian faith there is the assurance that the Love which is God is absolutely (and here it is appropriate to use that adverb) indefatigable and indefeasible—God will not ultimately be defeated, not because God coerces everything to do the divine will but because God is so inexhaustibly rich in resources that ways can be found to lure human creatures toward the realization of their own best good, which is the divine purpose for them and the contribution which they can make to God's own enjoyment. Yet we cannot use this as an alibi for our own failures and mistakes. What I am trying to show is that there is a basic certainty—someone has called it "cosmic security" resting upon "cosmic piety"—for humanity in their ethical endeavor; but at the same time there is the element of uncertainty or insecurity about human choices and actions. This is not a case of *Dieu la pardonnera, c'est son metier*—"it's going to be all right because God's job is to forgive everything." That would be a cheap and superficial view. Rather, it is a matter of the divine competence to accomplish unfailing good, because of and sometimes in spite of human recalcitrance.

The human vocation is to be a co-worker with the absolute Love that is God; to be with that Love as a "co-creator," in Whitehead's word, in all the relativity of our human situation and with the probability that mistake and failure will be part of our lot. This constitutes a calling which can bring out the best that is in humankind. My own theologoumenon, or theological opinion, on the matter is this: God wills and wants us to be full human beings, not slaves; God desires a conscious response, in full responsibility, to this invitation. God works constantly to make us mature, not knowing everything of course, but accepting our humanness and acting upon it. This is in some ways a frightening vocation, yet it is much better than if we were being treated as babies who must do what they are told and who can disclaim any responsibility for the doing of it.

I have spoken of taking thought. In the next chapter this will be considered in more detail; at this point, however, it is useful to say simply that the necessity for such thoughtful attention to ethical decision is obvious once we have seen that there are no ready-made answers and that we are obliged to choose among the various possibilities that the relativities of our lives inevitably offer. To a large extent our decisions will be in terms of more or less—*this* is more in line with the demands of love, *that* is less, as we may put it. This is why and how the absolute of love is available to us only in the relative this or that with which we must deal.

However, I return to the insistence on engagement or commitment. To say that we never have absolute certainty is not at all to say that we cannot act upon our decisions with utter dedication. In the ethical aspect of human experience such dedication is required, for the simple reason that nothing will ever be done at all if we permit ourselves only a reserved or qualified assent. This is where the insight of the existentialists is so valuable. They have shown that people move toward human fulfillment to the degree that they engage themselves with, or become committed to, a project that they have decided is the right one for them. Of course they may be wrong, and they should be ready to admit this if and when the fallacy is brought home. But unless they have given themselves, with all that they have, to some project, they will not be able to discern rightness or wrongness.

In religious language we say that we are meant to do the will of God, insofar as we have come honestly to see it, and to do it with our whole being. And the Christian insistence on what is known as "justification by grace through faith" has to do with just this demand. People cannot claim that they have exhaustive information about the details of the divine purpose. That is obvious enough. Yet their best insight into that purpose, for this or that specific occasion, is the guide with respect to what they are now to do. Having seen this immediate "ought," they will then give themselves to its execution, *fortiter* (as Luther said), "with all [their] heart and soul and mind and strength." At the same time they will know that something else is required. This is the commitment of themselves, of what they are doing, and of the consequences of their acts to the God whose character is *chesed*, or loving-mercy and acceptance, and also self-giving concern. In God they will find confidence to act and assurance that failures need not deflect the divine purpose; God can make even wrath turn to God's praise, to paraphrase

Psalm 76:10. In this way, in the moments of his or her decisive ethical decisions, a person is delivered from overmuch anxiety and from the fear that his or her single choice has ruined the movement toward a truly shared good, for God and for humankind.

Finally, we may be asked whether the stance we have taken does not destroy altogether the spontaneity that most of us feel should mark our lives. If we take thought and if we sense the real possibility of mistake and failure, shall we not then be inhibited and lose the freshness and eager responsiveness that we so much admire when we see it in others? But this does not necessarily follow, for it is just at this point that the value of habitual choices is demonstrated. The man or woman who has become accustomed to making decisions that are believed to be *for love*, in the direction of the one ethical absolute, will be able on succeeding occasions to act in a greater freedom. That person will begin to respond spontaneously to invitations for good which present themselves. Thereafter the taking thought, which is so necessary, will not amount to taking *anxious* thought—and it is the anxious kind of thought, the carefulness that makes one hesitate for too long a time between choices and that is constantly worried about every conceivable consequence, which causes the loss of freshness and spontaneity.

Francis of Assisi learned much through the decisions he made in the earlier days of his obedience to the requirement of love. Having thus learned, he was quick to recognize, and equally quick to act upon, later opportunities to express his loving concern. It might almost be said that his "ought" more and more became an "is." The direction of his life was so much toward the expression of love-in-action that he could not fail to respond to those persons and situations in which the possibility of acting in love presented themselves to him. If this was true of a Francis—and of Martin Luther King, Jr., in our own day—it was true a fortiori of the one whom Francis—and King—called Master. Jesus of Nazareth impresses us as one who indeed considered what God's will was for him; his hours of prayer and communion on the hillside and mountain were the times when he did this. But he also impresses us as one who acted spontaneously and with freshness and energy in his dealing with those who came to him for help or with whom he had to do in the many ways which the Gospel narratives paint for us. He did "the works of love," to use Kierkegaard's words, because he knew the absoluteness of the love of the heavenly Parent and because he was entirely surrendered to the doing of that Parent's will. In the idiom we have used elsewhere, he saw how the world really goes, he knew what was the grain of the universe; his vocation was to live and act in accordance with that. Nor was he delivered from the obligation to decide; had he been delivered from that obligation he would not have been truly human. Having decided, he proceeded to act—and in the end to act in such a way that his own death was required.

In John's Gospel there is a phrase worth our meditation: "Having loved his own who were in the world, he loved them *to the end* [John 13:1]." The Greek words behind "to the end" suggest a deeper meaning, however. What they tell us is just this: God loved them to the very limit of loving. For the phrase is *eis telos,* "to the end," in the sense of entire fulfillment and real completion. In other words, in Jesus the absolute of love was known in its fullness, so far as human existence allows; being known, it was then enacted, in equal fullness.

The central ethical principle and the only ethical absolute is "love divine, all loves excelling": it is God as Love and as Lover. Yet it speaks to human beings in their relativity as finite, not to say sinful, creatures. It also speaks to the circumstances in which they are placed. Thus we may claim that the "ought" in humankind is the imperative, the categorical imperative if you wish to use the Kantian phrase, to express that very love in the creaturely world. A Christian would add that this is both natural and inevitable, since men and women are being made toward the image of God, the image that in concrete manifestion in our midst is Jesus Christ himself.

5

Situation and Context in Ethics

5

Situation and Context in Ethics

Nowadays we hear a great deal of talk about the permissive society, a state of affairs in which some people think that there are no moral standards, no ethical principles imposed upon the citizens by law or by convention. Hence life is entirely unprincipled, the critics say. People do what they please without regard for decency, and young men and women are without any guidance as to how they should conduct their lives. This judgment upon which might better be styled an open society, which in many lands today most certainly will be found, is a violent reaction to what these critics feel to be libertinism—in fact, the antinomianism we referred to earlier.

To my mind it is particularly unfortunate that many who claim to speak for the Christian tradition are all too likely to join the ranks of those who decry the open society. They are bound to give the impression that they wish a return to "the good old days," as doubtless many would call them, in which ethical principles were enforced by law or required by the conventions of the social group that was then dominant. They forget that in those days there was a good deal of hypocrisy, a considerable number of people who could be counted on to speak in a high moral tone but were far from adopting any such standards in their own personal lives, not to speak of their acceptance of real social responsibility.

In truth, we have every reason to think that in a society where goodness (as it would be called) is imposed by law or demanded if one is to be accepted as a respectable citizen there is little genuine morality at all. Certainly such a society cannot be called an ethically principled society. Why do I say this? The answer is that only when there is freedom to decide for oneself, with responsibility assumed for the decisions made, can we talk about genuine morality or think that we are properly respecting the "ought" in human experience. We should not dream of calling an automaton, one of the robots in the play *R.U.R.*, between the wars, a moral being, nor should we describe it as behaving ethically.

For this reason, if for no other, those who are concerned about ethical behavior, above all those who profess the Christian attitude with respect to such behavior, ought to be ready to accept the fact that an open society is better than one that is closed. Furthermore, a degree of permissiveness permits experimentation, allows the possibility of ethical advance, quite as much as it opens the door to ethical confusion, and accords with the spirit of freedom that every responsible writer on ethics throughout history has insisted must be the mark of truly ethical decision.

We have already seen that the relativity found in human existence, both personal and social, does not necessarily mean that there is nothing which permanently endures as an ethical absolute. We have urged that there is indeed such an absolute: it is love-in-action, taken as the central ethical principle. Perhaps the contemporary rejection of the older conventional model of imposed morality is a justified reaction against the setting up of *other* supposed absolutes, not least the absolute of respectability associated with a predominantly bourgeois culture. As that culture has broken down in so many parts of the world, including

Great Britain and the United States where it is still *thought* to continue unquestioned but where it has in fact collapsed, the standards that it set up as not only desirable but enforceable by legal and social sanctions have shown themselves to have been idolatrous substitutions for the real absolute of love. And perhaps the virulence of the attacks upon the newer freedoms is to be explained as what in the British Isles has been styled the Puritan backlash—men and women who are dismayed at a freedom, which they themselves have never known, break out in violent denunciation of those who claim it and act upon it. One may even suspect that to some degree this is "sour grapes," unconscious envy of the new generation that demands and assumes a freedom that older people would have enjoyed but were prevented from knowing.

Obviously the situation can be confusing. For what we see about us is both the rejection of older conventions and the search for newer ethical principles. In that search there is bound to be uncertainty, not to say the experimentation which can seem like unawareness of the necessity for principles at all. Young people in particular find themselves in just such a condition. They have turned away from doing what the Joneses think right; they have asserted their own freedom to live as seems proper to them. But they have not yet found any self-validating principle upon which to base their notion of ethical conduct. I do not think that we help them very much when we only raise our voices in denunciation, try to impose a slightly updated version of the older ethics of externally imposed rule, and consider that these younger people, who at least have the merit of being honest, are lacking any ethical concern whatsoever.

The state of affairs that I have been describing provides the setting for recent efforts to work through the question of ethics once again, in a new spirit and with due recognition of the validity of the protest against the ethics of rule that was taken as eternally valid and was to be enforced either by law or by social convention. One of these attempts has been the much-discussed "situation ethics," first enunciated by Prof. Joseph Fletcher in a book of that name. Still another, in some respects more radical although firmly anchored in Christian conviction, has been contextual ethics. This has had its clearest expression in a book by Prof. Paul Lehmann entitled *Ethics in a Christian Context* (New York: Harper & Row, 1976). Both these writers are American, both are Christian (Fletcher an Anglican, Lehmann a Presbyterian), and both are keenly aware of the changes that have taken place in the attitude of large numbers of younger people. Furthermore, both are concerned to assert, as in this book we have done, that love is the central ethical principle and the only ethical absolute in a world of process and change marked by the relativity that is inevitable in such a world.

In *Situation Ethics* (Philadelphia: Westminster Press, 1966), Fletcher takes with the utmost seriousness the point we have argued throughout this book—that the situation in which a decision is made or an act done inevitably determines largely if not wholly the ethical quality of that decision or act. Things do not take place in a vacuum; they always have their context. And the context in which they take place has much to do with the content of what occurs. The ethical appropriateness of a decision or act, therefore, will have to be understood in a way different from that which might obtain if we could abstract this from the concrete situation. So also it will be understood in a way different from that which might obtain if we had some entirely absolute and conclusive dictate that could be applied in all circumstances, regardless of when or what they were.

The title of Lehmann's book indicates that he is specifically interested in arguing for the *Christian* context of ethical behavior. His point is that within this context there is a different slant on the matter, since Christian faith introduces significantly new considerations. But of course his argument could be extended to show that *any* context, both of situation and of conviction, will qualify the ethical decision or act. Who I am, where I stand, what are my deepest convictions, and not least the kind of community to which I belong—all these are highly relevant and require attention when appraisal is made of the way in which I have chosen and the way in which I have acted.

It is not my purpose to discuss at length the arguments of these two distinguished authorities. I have cited them for two reasons. The first reason is that they are interesting indications of a general tendency in ethical thinking away from complete fixity of standards and toward an awareness of what I call relativity in the whole matter of choice and behavior. The second is that both Fletcher and Lehmann put enormous stress on love as *the* ethical principle. Indeed, Fletcher puts *all* his stress on love; it is for him, as for us in this book, the only absolute. Lehmann qualifies this a little, since he is more dependent upon the variety of approach found in the earlier biblical and the later Evangelical Protestant portrayal of ethics; yet in the end it is unquestionably true that for him love is the ultimate and permanent principle.

Of course I could have cited many other writers, but I chose these because of their clear Christian allegiance. It is not only the nonreligious or non-Christians who take the newer attitude, then; within the Christian community itself that attitude is accepted. As John Robinson urged in *Honest to God* (Philadelphia: Westminster Press, 1963) and even more plainly in the later *Christian Morals Today* (Philadelphia: Westminster Press, 1964), the Christian world itself has been undergoing a revolution in the matter of ethics quite as much as in theology. That revolution, however, is not a destructive one that would entirely overthrow or deny the past. Rather, as Dr. Robinson urges, it is a business of radical insight, using the word radical in its proper Latin derivation, "roots" or "to the roots," a penetration to the essential core of meaning that the inherited tradition has been trying to get at, whether in theological statement or in ethical affirmation. In each instance that root meaning is *love*: God is primarily Love rather than power or abstract being or moral dictator; and sound ethics is the awareness of love as the absolute principle, with a morality that builds upon love rather than upon fixed law or precise code.

For our own part we can say that the only viable possibility for a contemporary ethic is in exactly this direction. And we may now examine the implications of such an ethic, so far as concrete practice is concerned.

In the first place, an ethic of love will require a reordering of priorities, in the sense of what procedures are to be followed when a decision is made. There is the requirement of taking thought, so far as may be possible in any given instance, about what are clearly the factors in the case. We have already noted this and have pointed out that it does not deny or make impossible the genuine spontaneity of the agent. But we need also to recognize that among these factors we must include the probable consequences of our decisions. Plainly these cannot be known in exact detail; there is bound to be a considerable element of the unexpected in the results of any choice made or act done. Nonetheless, granted this, we are obliged to take due account of the *likely* results, so far as we can imagine them or guess them. Without this, the ethical will become the merely preferential—or at least will tend that way.

Included in the consequences is always the way in which what is decided will affect for good or ill those with whom we live or the wider human community of which we are a part. In a societal world, where each occasion influences every other occasion, it would be going against the grain of things to decide for oneself as if one's own immediate wishes were the single criterion. Love is sharing; and the works of love are those acts that bring about more mutuality, deeper community, and fuller participation for all.

If I am a Christian, there is still another point that needs to be emphasized. A Christian can only decide and act *as* a Christian, no matter what sort of situation there is to deal with. Patently, many who call themselves by the Christian name are in truth Christian *only* in name. In that case they can hardly be expected to decide and act *as* Christians. Yet for the person who calls himself or herself Christian there is the obligation to consider seriously the imperatives of that profession; and we may be thankful that in recent years there is much less diffused "cultural Christianity"—adherence only because it is the socially acceptable thing—and much more concerned and dedicated Christian allegiance. Here too is the reason for a growing feeling that a basic requirement in Christian education today is the deepening of conscious Christian discipleship among young and old. Those who are thus growing in the reality of their Christian belonging will inevitably bring to bear on their ethical existence the specifically Christian insight into how things go in the world. And that will have its profound effect on how they look at themselves, at the world, at the concrete choices they must make, and in the final resort at the results of those choices upon the future of God's working in the world.

What am I? I am a personalized movement toward realization of possibility, which for a human is toward becoming a lover who both reflects and represents the divine Love. What is the world? It is the when and the where in which the cosmic Love is at work, largely active through creaturely agents. What are my choices for? They are for the more adequate expression, in any and every way, of such divine Love humanly instrumental for greater good. And what about the results of those choices? They either contribute to, or they serve as deflections from, the very same divine Love in its creaturely manifestations.

Professor Moltmann writes in the essay from which we have already quoted, "Human life is accepted, loved, and experienced life" (p. 102). He is distinguishing here between genuine human life and simple biological existence, and he urges that when and where there is not this accepting, loving, and experiencing we are not dealing with anything truly human at all, but merely with a vital phenomenon. By acceptance he means the mutuality to which we have often referred; by loving he means the way in which that mutuality is characterized by a positive concern and caring; and by experiencing he means a depth of existence that we would characterize as zest or intensity. The mark of genuine human life for him is its capacity to exist with diversity or difference, in conscious acceptance of difference and contrast, with the pain and the joy that this will bring, and the "containing" of such diversity—sometimes almost to the point of contradiction—within an "interest" (again in his own word) which "takes part in other life" and refuses to indulge in "indifference and apathy."

With this definition of human life, Moltmann presents a serious criticism of, indeed an attack upon, industrial society as we know it today. He sees in it a loss of human identity, a kind of anthill existence, where lives are prolonged by medical knowledge but where life does not appear to be much worth living. Unhappily he does not stress, as in my judgment he should have, the movement toward a more open (and permissive) society, as well as other trends that take his critical point but that are also acting to correct the depersonalizing character of mass humanity and mass society. One of these correctives is the kind of thinking and teaching given by a Fletcher and a Lehmann and a Robinson, who are only three representatives of what I venture to think is the most vigorous ethical school today.

We may be grateful, however, for Moltmann's definition of what it means to be human; and it will be apparent how closely his definition approaches the position argued in this book. It will also be apparent that his definition carries with it the ethical corollary that human "oughtness" must be in the direction of more acceptance, more love, and more genuine experience in depth, with the adventurous quality which redeems it from mere acquiescence in a static code that cannot reckon with novelty when it makes its appearance. When we take thought and when we consider consequences, a significant—maybe *the* significant—question will be the degree to which this reading of "ought" is central to the picture.

In such a way of interpreting ethical obligation, the high

probability of error must be admitted. We have done this, to be sure, in our comments about mistakes in grasping the full situation, thanks to the finitude of humankind; and we have insisted upon failure on the part of people to act up to their best knowledge, as well as upon the unfortunate way in which unexpected and unplanned-for consequences often make their appearance. If there is no absolute infallibility in moral decision, there is also no absolute certainty about moral consequences. But there is something else, and that is the reality of human perversity and cupidity.

That too has been mentioned, but only in passing. Now it is time for us to look more carefully at this disagreeable fact. The theological word for it is sin, a word that in our own time, alas, has been so much damaged that it is of little use in ordinary discussion. If it does not suggest something to do with sexual behavior—"living in sin" immediately implies for many some sort of sexual misconduct, such as living together without benefit of clergy or of civil license—it calls to mind violation of an externally imposed law. So sin is usually taken to be breaking the rules or breaking the commandments. Its basic meaning, however, as a study of the scriptural material in both Old and New Testaments will tell us, is quite different. In the biblical understanding of it, sin is essentially a violation of an intended relationship between God and humankind and hence between one person and another. It has its corollaries, of course; the breaking of those relationships leads to all manner of subsequent evil. But the latter are the results of the former, if the Bible is to be trusted.

How does sin arise then? The answer here is that it comes into being when people disregard the divine purpose of shared life and seek for their own personal aggrandizement. As a matter of fact, there is no such *thing* as sin anyway; there are only *people* who assert themselves in such a fashion that they break the proper mutual and responsible relationship they were intended to have, both with God and with their neighbor. They do this precisely because of cupidity, which is a proud assertion of selfhood over and against everyone else. This is the perversity in human existence.

And it is pervasive. Again in theological language, there is the fact of "original sin." This does not mean that human existence is radically evil, down at its very roots, but it does mean that wherever people exist they exist as inheritors of a state of affairs in which through long millennia of self-centered decisions (and the actions consequent upon such decisions) they are in the unhappy position of finding choice for true good—that is, for the loving and shareable—so hard as to be almost impossible for them. Unfortunately, a good deal of conventional theology has talked about original sin in almost sexual terms, misrepresenting the meaning of the line in Psalm 51:5, "in sin did my mother conceive me." This line has nothing to do with coition; it is a way of saying that anything and everything done by humankind is to some degree distorted by the cupidity or false self-centeredness just mentioned. We should do better to speak of a social, or sociological, communication of such distortion.

The persistence of this condition produces alienation of those who are its victims from their truest human intention, from other people, and from God's purpose for them. What is more, it also produces a sense of estrangement from all three. It is easy enough to see how this is manifested if we take love as our clue. Since I am intended to realize my potentiality for life-in-love, my cupidity or self-centeredness alienates me from that realization. Since I am intended to live in deep relationship with others, this self-regard alienates me from such a relationship. Since I am to be in the image of God who is Love, overweening self-assertion is alienation from that image. The same thing may be seen with respect to estrangement: my cupidity estranges me from my possible existence in self-giving, it estranges me from my neighbors, whose good I am intended to seek, and it estranges me from God's love because I am concerning myself no longer with God's purpose but with my own ends.

So much then for the background and the definition of humankind's perversity and cupidity. We all are caught up in it, however much we may pretend that we are free of it. But we must ask ourselves whether this fact about us does not make impossible *any* ethical obedience, *any* response to the "ought" in human existence. The answer to this question is found in the Christian theological tradition—unlikely as that may seem to many of our contemporaries who reject without examination what that tradition has to tell us.

Two points are made there. The first is that God gives grace, the divine favorable and empowering strength, to God's children. To those who are ready to open themselves to it, this grace is an enabling agency. It does not guarantee that all our decisions will be correct, or that all our acts will produce the right results. But it will *aid* us in what *The Book of Common Prayer* collect for the ninth Sunday after Trinity affirms: granting us "the spirit to think and do always such things as are right"—to think and hence to discern; and to do or act upon that discernment.

The second point is that such grace is not limited to those who are within the specifically Christian community. Unfortunately some have assumed this to be the case, but the mainstream of Christian thought has spoken otherwise. In differing expression, that mainstream has been continually aware of the wider operation of the Holy Spirit throughout the creation, or of the general working of the "unincarnate Word," or of what John Calvin named "common grace" without which no one lives and because of which the human condition is prevented from going utterly amok. In other words, no one anywhere (whether a Christian or a Hindu or a humanist or an agnostic or an atheist) exists entirely apart from God and from the working of God in his or her life.

As we have seen in every other instance, we find our best approach here by seeing love as our key. Within Christian existence and within all other existence too, there is a pervasive feeling that love is absolute. Perhaps this absolute love is not consciously seen as grounded in the nature of things; to many, not least in our own time, the love about which we are talking may appear to be a purely human phenomenon with nothing in the cosmos that corresponds to it. Yet we need not trouble ourselves too much about that conscious and rational attitude; what matters most is not the ideas people may have about such metaphysical questions, important as these are, but whether or not there is within them such a deep and troubling recognition of love as central and essential.

Nor is it only a discernment of the centrality of love; it is also the experience of finding oneself empowered in loving. How this happens we may often have difficulty in saying; but that it does happen is the witness of the great artists, poets, scientists, musicians, and thinkers, and also of the ordinary man or woman who feels somehow strengthened in loving, having once allowed himself or herself to be opened up to love. It may be too that a hard core of selfhood is now and again shattered by the presence of other persons, by causes that make their demands upon an individual, or by imperatives to act that come by some unknown means.

Nowhere is our present contention more vividly illustrated than in the extraordinary fashion in which many younger people in our own day are stressing the reality of love, its enormous power in human existence, and the possibility of committing one's whole existence to such love. In earlier days the word love was often a somewhat weak word, as I have said before. But with such younger people nowadays the word has become an astonishingly strong word. Their mode of acting upon love may appear strange, even outrageous, to their elders; but we cannot deny their commitment, their conviction, and their willingness to act in love, so far as they are able. In the situations in which they find themselves, with their limitations and inhibitions, they yet see that love is absolute; in the contexts that are theirs they accept love as the central ethical principle. And if they can find their way into a definitely *Christian* context, such as Professor Lehmann describes, they know a remarkable empowering that gives them courage to do brave and adventurous things. I wish I had space here to list some of these, but I can mention only the single dedication they have shown to racial understanding and to the ending of unjust and indecent military conflict even when to take these stands has brought them condemnation as unpatriotic, subversive, and ungrateful to their country and class.

6

Personal and Social Ethical Questions

6

Personal and Social Ethical Questions

*Our discussion of the "ought" in humankind, with the conclu*sion that love is the central ethical principle and the one ethical absolute, has been focused on the theoretical side: we have been talking about the basis of ethics, the general approach that is now replacing a more legalistic attitude, and questions of a quasi-philosophical and theological sort. Some readers may wonder how all this works itself out in concrete and practical ways, in the particular decisions that people must make and in the behavior that such decisions produce.

In this chapter we shall illustrate our position by taking one or two instances in which the new approach has been, or may be, put to work. In the sphere of personal relations we shall look at changing sexual ethics; in that of social relationships we shall concern ourselves with problems of group conflict, such as those between labor and management or between persons of different races who somehow must live together and discover a modus vivendi. I make no claim that my discussion will be definitive, but I believe that by giving these two areas serious attention we can see the value of the insistence on love as central ethical principle, along with some of the questions or problems that may still remain.

Everybody knows that sexual ethics have changed greatly during the past half century. In part this change has its origin in the much relaxed hold of traditional religious belief on younger people. Not too long ago the Christian faith was fairly widely accepted, at least in a superficial way, and with that acceptance went an ethical attitude that nowadays we should style puritanical. This was certainly the case in lands where the so-called Protestant ethic was dominant: Great Britain, the Anglo-Saxon countries of what is now the British Commonwealth, the United States, and elsewhere. In Catholic lands the puritanical ethic had nowhere near as much influence; hence the somewhat "superior" fashion in which Italians, Frenchmen, and even Spaniards (although in Spanish lands Catholic Jansenist influence often brought a puritanical ethic into prominence) were dismissed by those who believed the Protestant ethic to be indubitably moral and even indubitably Christian! A great deal of attention was given in Protestant lands to the Old Testament teaching on ethics, often without due regard for the qualifications made in that position by later Judaism and by Christian insight.

Perhaps we could sum up the older sexual ethic in this way: Men and women are indeed possessed of sexual desires, and the equipment that makes their expression possible. But sex is not to be much discussed; if it is not a nasty subject, it must at least be kept a secret matter. The purpose of sex is the procreation of children; that is, it is essentially nature's reproductive device for ensuring the continuation of the human race. Any pleasure derived from sexual contacts is secondary to its main purpose and "nice people" will not dwell on that pleasurable aspect (indeed, for many the pleasurable aspect was thought to be associated with "immoral sex," or what went on in the brothel or between persons who were indulging in illicit relationships outside of or apart from marriage).

Marriage was established by God in the natural order as the means for giving human sexuality a proper setting. Premarital or extramarital sexual activity was frowned upon as being wrong, while sexuality between persons of the same sex (homosexuality) was outrageous, abnormal, unnatural, and sinful. In this context, romantic love between persons of differing gender or the same gender was a subject that could not be avoided, but on the whole it was looked upon as less truly human than a settled relationship in marriage, in which a shared life, the rearing of a family, and mutual support and care were central, rather than the actual depth of feeling between the parties. This meant that divorce was not socially respectable, more particularly on the part of the woman. A divorced woman was often thought to have been unable to sustain the marriage relationship, and she was either condemned as of doubtful morality or pitied for her failure to keep her husband.

Sexual experimentation on the part of children, adolescents, and young people was taken to be immoral too. Some license was given the young man, since he might be expected to sow his wild oats before he engaged himself for life with the woman of his choice. This was sometimes condoned but it was not an accepted aspect of life. As to autoerotic sexuality, especially on the part of boys, the attitude was one of suppression and fear; masturbation was supposed to be psychologically and physiologically dangerous, producing insanity, instability, skin ailments like acne, or permanent physical malfunctioning and illness.

Delight in sexual expression, the seeking of emotional and physical satisfaction through such expression, frank discussion of the subject, and liberty in decisions about sexual desires and their implementation in act—all these were considered to be damaging both to the person and to the society of which he or she was a part.

Now it is obvious that people did not always behave in the ways which such an attitude would indicate. There was an astounding amount of hypocrisy, not least on the part of the males of the time. And there was a great deal of what was officially regarded as immoral behavior at every level of society, perhaps most frequently among those who were in high places and whose conduct belied the high moral tone of their public utterances. I think that anybody who (like myself) lived as a boy or young man in the pre-World War I period would agree that the picture I have drawn of the general line of thought about sex is an accurate one.

Of course, things are very different today. It is hardly necessary to portray the contemporary scene with respect to sexual attitudes and the sexual mores of the generations that have grown up since, say, the late twenties or thirties of this century. Nor is it necessary to indicate how the relaxation during those years has been followed by an attitude of greater acceptance today, when freedom is taken for granted by vast numbers to enjoy the pleasure sex can give, and when the question of principles in sexual behavior is so open. Two points may be made, however. One is that thanks to the Pill and other means of preventing conception of children, sexual relationships no longer are seen primarily as a matter of reproduction; as Professor Moltmann observes in the essay from which I have already quoted, "sexual union for love can [now] be separated from that for reproduction." He notes also that "the begetting and birth of a child has thereby become a moral and social question" (p. 102). The other point is that sexual experimentation and experience before marriage, and even apart from marriage, is regarded as being much less significant, as wrong or evil, than the denial of all sexual expression to those who are not already married. In this connection also there is little if any condemnation of autoerotic practices, especially by the young, while homosexual relationships are more and more regarded as right and proper for those who wish them and who enjoy them.

Some think that this vast change in attitude and in behavior represents the end of all morality. Those who take this view can only condemn and attack what they see as an abdication of ethical principle and a demonstration that civilization is on its way to complete ruination. The extreme conservative

Christian says that the end of all things is at hand, a sign of which is considered to be widespread immorality, the loss of all moral standards, and the acceptance by the public of indecency, libertinism, and completely unprincipled behavior. Less extreme people are disturbed and troubled, although they do not know what to say or do in such a situation. There is confusion and worry, sometimes dismay and fear for the future.

The reader will know that I cannot take this negative attitude. But this does not mean that I do not recognize both the desirability and the necessity of guidelines in sexual behavior. These guidelines are related, of course, to the older rules or commandments, insofar as the latter suggest how our ancestors understood ethical obligation and responsibility. Their function, however, is not to inhibit sexual expression but to indicate the general direction of truly fulfilling sexuality. For one thing, these ancient regulations point to the truth that entirely uncontrolled sexual expression is damaging to those who engage in it and to the society to which they belong. Some ordering of sexual life is necessary if human life is not to collapse into sheer anarchy. But to say this is not to say that modes of sexual activity upon which our ancestors frowned must for that very reason, and that alone, be considered wicked and perverse.

We might illustrate this by the fairly general acceptance today of some measure of sexual experimentation by adolescents. As a young man of my acquaintance put this, the only thing that can be wrong with such experimentation is its possibly becoming the *only* interest of the girl or boy. In that case, sexual activity would be so dominant in the life of a person that it would be disproportionate; after all, there is much else which any young person must engage in, and there are many areas of experience—and experiment—that are not in any immediate sense sexual at all. Or we might speak of the newer way of looking at masturbatory practices. Most of the damage these may occasion comes not from the physical acts but from the fears that are awakened by well-intentioned but quite uninformed elders. We now know that masturbation, as such, is harmless. It cannot damage psychologically save when it becomes obsessive; and nobody can masturbate to excess (as many used to phrase it) because physiologically the limits are inevitably given by the body itself.

I prefer, however, to put the stress here not on masturbation and youthful experimentation but on the increasing awareness of the propriety of homosexual relationships, including physical contacts, for the 10 percent of the population who are included in the category of homosexual persons. If human sexuality is not itself an evil thing, if its purpose is not primarily the reproduction of the race but the establishment of union at the deepest and most inclusive level, and if at the same time a reasonably large proportion of the human race are (for whatever reasons) able only to find love with members of their own gender a satisfying and fulfilling matter, there are no sensible grounds for rejecting it as evil. In another book (*Time for Consent* [London: SCM Press, 1967]) I argued this point; and more recently I have included a chapter on this subject, considering among other factors the supposed taboo on homosexuality found in the Jewish and Christian scriptures, in my *Making Sexuality Human* ([New York: The Pilgrim Press, 1970], pp. 59–68). But I have also suggested in that book and in its sequel, *Love and Control in Sexuality* (New York: The Pilgrim Press, 1974), the "controls" that love itself establishes for the homosexual, controls that are as much given in homosexual contacts as they are in heterosexual ones.

My purpose here is not to repeat my arguments in those books, but only to indicate the controls that the central ethical principle of love make obvious to any responsible person. These controls are five, as it seems to me: (1) All sexual contacts must be mutual and not selfish or entirely self-gratifying, because love itself is in giving and receiving. (2) They must be in the direction of a personalizing rather than a depersonalizing of the participants, because love is always a personalizing agency.

(3) They must be the kind of sharing that helps and builds up, not that which is cruel or hurting, because love always heals and edifies (in the primary meaning of that word, building up or soundly developing). (4) They must be ordinate or proportionate, as we have already indicated, because love is expressed in total relationships and not exclusively in the specifically genital one. (5) They must be responsible, with consideration of the self-esteem of each partner, because love is always concerned with the welfare of others and with the consequences of that which one does to them, with them, or for them.

I believe that these corollaries of love, taken as the ethical absolute, commend themselves to men and women as being sensible and proper; they also commend themselves because they are precisely what I have said of them—they are the inevitable implication of love itself, not imposed from some other sphere but integral to love itself. And it is worth our remarking that if we have come to emphasize, as we must, the conjunctive or unitive nature of all human sexuality, rather than its secondary nature as procreational, we can move toward a truly ethical understanding in which "ought" no longer assumes an exclusively negative aspect but is seen as primarily positive in its directives. While our illustration has been taken from the homosexual and his sexual expression, exactly the same point may be made about heterosexual sexual behavior. In my judgment, the newer openness and freedom in the sexual area is all to the good. Despite the commonly made criticism by those who still hold to an older ethical attitude, this openness and freedom are far from representing a collapse into immorality and ethical chaos. On the contrary, they may be seen as a move toward a more sound morality and a more searching and demanding ethic.

A positive appreciation of the goodness of sex, an equally positive acceptance of the pleasure it can give—as a friend of mine has said, "Sex should be fun, and there's nothing wrong about that!"—and with these a rejection of repressive rules if these exist only for their own sake and do not contribute to positive appreciation and acceptance: here is nothing unethical. Far from it. Here is a basis upon which an ethic centered in love, expressed in freedom, and entailing genuine responsibility may be built. I believe that precisely this sort of ethic will emerge out of the confusion of our own day.

When we turn to the social side of human conduct, much the same may be seen. The two areas with which we shall concern ourselves here are labor and management, on the one hand, and racial relationships, on the other. Here again we have witnessed an enormous change both in attitude and in behavior. We also see the same kind of fears that we observed with respect to sexual behavior. There are those who wish to maintain the older combative situation between the wage-earner and artisan and the boss or manager. There are also those who think that the only way to treat the racial problem, as they call it, is by separation with equality (the latter nowadays replaces, among conservative people, the older idea of special privilege), avoiding the mingling of the races or the sharing of schools and residential areas. But it is apparent that neither of these positions will work any longer.

In an increasingly tight-knit society, and despite the proper feeling that the rights of both workers and managers are to be preserved, there is growing understanding that the two must learn how to get along together, how to cooperate for their own good and for the common good, and how to establish at least a modicum of friendliness. Similarly, it is hopeless these days to attempt to continue policies of segregation of races, even under the banner of "difference, but with equality of opportunity." Interrelationships, mingling, and shared life in the community are inevitable, and this is coming about through the pressures of urban life as well as through the demands made by the less privileged races for their full part and place in society.

Suppose we take love as the central ethical principle. How can this have anything to do with labor-management problems and with race relations?

Our answer must be along these lines: There is no possibility of working out the difficulties between those who work and those for whom they work unless there is the spirit to do just this. When that spirit is absent, no amount of negotiation will be of much use, nor will the agreements that are made between the two parties have any enduring value. Surely the history of industrialized society bears this out. On the one hand, there have been owners of business concerns who have had no interest save in increased profits for themselves and their shareholders. Equally, there have been labor leaders who have sought only to augment pay by squeezing the other side as much as possible. We may sympathize most with the workers—in fact, I myself do—but this does not alter the simple fact that all too often in the past they have entered into negotiations with no real spirit of sympathy, especially without much sympathy for the consumer who is indubitably the victim of price increases. I realize that what has just been written can be dismissed as too *simpliste*, too naive. And I acknowledge that there are enormous economic problems that only experts can intelligently face and handle. At the same time, I am sure that what I have written is not too far off the mark; and I am even more convinced that one of the most important developments in recent years has been the greater willingness of both sides to approach the conference table in a spirit more open to compromise, more aware of problems on both sides, and more ready to see that the general public is seriously involved in whatever agreements are to be made.

Likewise in the matter of race relations. The demands for justice are properly put forward by Black leaders, and those demands deserve the support of every right-thinking person. On the other hand, common sense requires us to see that much of the white opposition to full equality springs from a fear that jobs will be lost, "nice neighborhoods" altered, and educational standards lowered. These fears are essentially stupid and without real grounds. Yet they do exist. And because they exist, they must be met and shown to be false or mistaken. There is only one way in which this can happen, and that is through a spirit of conciliation and cooperation. After all, the race question is much more than a matter of justice for persons of any color; it is a matter of a personal awareness of men and women who belong to another race. That awareness is nothing other than love in action. It is expressed in willingness to meet, talk with, come to know, and eventually even to like those who have a black skin or a white skin. In this connection I shall never forget a Black student of mine who told me years ago that what he most wanted, what he would most appreciate from his teachers and from other students, all of whom were white, was a tangible manifestation that they looked upon him not so much as a Black man but as another human being, a brother just like them in deep personality traits and yearnings and desires. But to adopt that attitude requires love, the sort of openness, mutuality, giving and receiving, and readiness to work together about which we have been talking in this book.

The acceptance of love as the absolute will not solve all the problems that our relative human situations present to us. These must be met and dealt with by whatever techniques, civil laws, and conditions are obviously required in the particular instances in view. But acceptance of love as the central ethical principle will bring into those situations the spirit that can use all these techniques, laws, and conditions in a fashion that will promote genuine cooperation and fellowship in the common human enterprise. Basically, that is what matters most.

There is another area of human life, in which I myself have spent many years. That is education; and in my case, it has been education at the university and postgraduate levels. I must confess that I have known far too many teachers who have regarded their students in an entirely impersonal way, looking at them as if they were simply *there*, to be exposed to what was being taught them but with no real desire for a contribution from their side. I have also known students who thought of their teachers as ridiculous old men or women or as persons concerned merely to indulge in the game of indoctrination. Both attitudes are hardly likely to do much to improve academic relationships, nor are they likely to make life in a university more pleasant for everybody. On the contrary, they exacerbate the problems of faculty-student relations and have nothing constructive to offer.

As I write I think of something else, however. I think of a man who has been high in the councils of the university of which I am now a member. For some years he was in charge of the discipline of the institution, occupying that office during one of our most trying periods, when student protest at "faculty indifference" was at its height and when this problem was made worse by a failure of local law enforcement agencies to understand the significance of the then somewhat serious drug problem among certain groups of students. My friend is a man of academic integrity; he is also a man of deep Christian conviction, with a genuine concern for other persons and an interest in their welfare. By his spirit, by his willingness to spend untold hours with young men and women in trouble, by his patience and understanding, above all by his readiness to act as a channel between them and the higher boards of the university, he was largely responsible for easing the situation and for establishing sufficient rapport for a joint committee to meet, discuss, and present recommendations that would maintain the academic requirements and the need for order but also allow greater student participation in university affairs, representation on governing bodies, and even a considerable measure of student-controlled discipline.

Had my friend not been there, I do not know what might have happened; but because he *was* there, a possibility of cooperation was given that was much more important than any particular measures simple justice would have demanded. For the problem was not merely one of justice in an abstract sense. Like all major human problems, including the two to which we have just been referring (labor-management and race relations), the personal element was central. The only way in which the problem could be handled constructively was through the expression of love in action; this my friend did, and the results were extraordinary. Doubtless they were also largely unrecognized, so far as many faculty members and students were concerned. But my friend would not bother about anything of that sort—*his* interest was only to act in such a way that necessary reforms were introduced and significant changes made in routine, so that we could all get on with our work in a friendly and mutually helpful fashion.

Tough bargaining, honest statement of views, frank facing of differences, and all the other worldly factors in human relationships between groups and classes and nations are essential, of course. But in every case they are relative to the problems being faced. The one abiding absolute is the spirit of love, however this may express itself, under whatever disguises and through whatever means. Without that spirit, our best efforts will fail, often very soon, certainly in the long run.

That is the way the world goes. I return here to my constantly repeated affirmation that the deepest and most enduring reality is a thrust or drive toward mutuality—toward love expressed in finite ways and through finite persons, who also, alas! are defective and distorted in their judgments and marked by the trait of self-centeredness and cupidity. But as the human race has gone on, more and more of its most profound thinkers have come to believe, with all their hearts and with all their minds too, that love is stronger than force, that persuasion is more effective than coercion, and that mutuality is more satisfying than conflict. In every part of the world, from China and India to Europe and the Americas, this belief is found—and found increasingly. Sadly, it is a belief that frequently receives only lip service, but where it is given concrete expression in decisions and in actions it has demonstrated its efficacy. Those who call themselves Christians are invited to show just such an attitude and behave in just that way. They are not alone in doing this, for (as Dr. Macquarrie has shown) what used to be called general revelation confirms their belief, and men of goodwill in all parts of the world are in agreement with it.

I permit myself a final comment, in response to some reader who may feel that an approach such as we have taken in this book does not provide the sort of specific ethical directive that can cover each and every decision and its consequent act. My comment begins with a quotation from Aristotle (*Ethics*, trans. J.A.K. Thompson [New York: Penguin Books, 1955], 1. 3. 27–28): "It is the mark of the educated man . . . that in every subject he looks for only so much precision (*akribeia*) as its nature permits." Whatever may be the case with scientific research and experiment, academic theorizing, and logical argument if it is clear that the ethical life—and much else, for that matter—is *not* a subject that permits or makes possible detailed and precise directives. There is always an element of doubt, of uncertainty, of greater or less, better or worse, in these areas of human experience. Would we really wish it otherwise? I argue that we should not, however convenient it might seem to be if it were so. Our human existence and with it our ethical awareness are altogether too all-encompassing and yet also too inevitably risky to make us want everything laid on the line, with no obscure corners, dimly discerned consequences, or open-ended attitudes.

Luther's famous dictum that we are "to sin boldly, but believe even more boldly" is relevant here. By "sin boldly" the Reformer intended to indicate that whatever choices we make will doubtless be more or less imperfect, defective, and partial. So be it; this is the inescapable condition of creaturely existence. But we can also believe more boldly in that we can put our entire trust and wholehearted confidence in the cosmic Love that is reflected (however inadequately) in our human urge to love. Thus in our ethical decisions, as elsewhere, we are "justified by grace through faith": the cosmic Lover accepts and uses even our imperfect and imprecise decisions, and also accepts *us* who make and implement those necessarily uncertain judgments with the specific acts that follow upon them.

7

The Ethical Norm: Love in a Processive World

7

The Ethical Norm: Love in a Processive World

How shall I close this book?

I have thought long and hard about this question and I have concluded that I can best bring our discussion to an end by offering a summary statement of a faith that appears to me viable in the modern world—a faith that is continuous with the Christian past of which we are the inheritors but that reckons very seriously with the new insights that have come to us during the past century. And once I have done that, I can reaffirm the ethical stance for which I have been arguing, basing it upon the vision of the world, humankind, and God which this faith provides.

Christian faith has two *foci* of deepest concern. One is God and the other is humankind. But these are not seen in total separation one from the other. Indeed, the Christian conviction that, in Jesus Christ, God and humankind are inextricably united makes any such separation impossible. There is more to it than that, however. In biblical thought, more particularly in the New Testament but also in the Old Testament, which the Christian community took over as the record of the *praeparatio evangelica* —the preparation for the gospel of Jesus Christ—God is never portrayed without due emphasis upon divine activity in the world. Jewish faith, and in consequence Christian faith, does not look to some remote and self-contained metaphysical first cause or essential being who might be thought about in isolation from the creation. On the contrary, whatever is said about God is said in terms of God's presentness and God's providential operation in that creation.

Humankind also is never seen as entirely separated from God. There is some working of the divine in men and women and in their history or social experience, however dimly this may be known and however defective may be the response to it. Nor does the working of God necessarily become a matter of conscious awareness on the part of humankind. There is an element of incognito, as I should wish to call it, about that working, so that God is not obvious. As Charles Hartshorne would put it, God makes things make themselves; and what is visible to us is that creaturely "making themselves." The divine must be inferred; or better, known by insight that penetrates deep into the creaturely working and discerns there something more than creaturely although not contrary to or against the creaturely.

Unhappily, the way in which both God and humanity have been pictured in a good deal of Christian thinking and teaching has overlooked the points I have made in the two preceding paragraphs. Moreover, an even more unhappy aspect of that thinking and teaching has been a readiness to model God after the abstract mode of certain elements in Greek philosophy rather than after the concrete model given in what Whitehead called "the brief Galilean vision." In saying this I am pointing to the patent fact that often God has been set up as the absolute exception to everything else known to us—is regarded as supranatural in what amounts to a *contra*-natural fashion. God is the cause of everything else and is responsible for everything else, even (in some theologies at any rate) for the evil, both natural and moral, that appears in the world. God is absolute in that there is no relationship *ad extra* that is essential to the divine nature; God subsists as the essence that exists from itself alone and to which nothing else can make any contribution. Hence God's transcendence has been interpreted as God's utter aseity —a completely self-contained and self-sufficient existence.

Such a picture of God is hardly the one with which religious people actually work in their concrete experience. It puts God far off, *so* self-contained, *so* self-sufficient, that the creation seems an irrelevance. No ordinary religious person has thought this to be the case, nor have the theologians in their practical religious experience thought it. For such people God is at hand, inviting and valuing what creation can do toward the fulfillment of the divine purpose. Above all, God is enriched or impoverished by what goes on in that creation. God rejoices with those who rejoice, suffers with those who suffer. Nothing else can surpass God, since God is perfect in goodness and love. But God can surpass even God, in that at some future moment God can be more fully expressed and more fully satisfied than at a previous moment—otherwise prayer, worship, and loyal discipleship or cooperation with God would also be an irrelevance.

But the place where the conventional picture has been most at fault is in its focusing attention on God as "power and might," to use the words an interdenominational liturgical committee has proposed to translate the eucharistic Sanctus' "Lord God of hosts." In light of the event of Jesus Christ, not to mention the insight of such prophets as Hosea, many parts of Isaiah, and Jeremiah, one would have assumed that the stress should be laid on God's nature as love-in-action, on God's "persuasion" (in Whitehead's words), rather than on "power and might." But the human mind sometimes seems to be almost incurably power mad, at least in its thinking about deity; and the theological emphasis has been placed there. Yet certainly the distinctively Christian affirmation has to do with the love of God which was in Christ Jesus our Lord. If that affirmation is true, then power-as such, in the sense of sheer coercion, cannot be taken as the primary aspect of the divine. Love is primary—"God is love," says 1 John—and whatever needs to be said about God's power must be said with that in mind. Christian thinking would have done better if it had subordinated power to love, if it had talked about God's power as always and entirely the sort of power that love can exercise. Aristotle, of all people, once spoke of "the power which the loved one exercises on the lover," and we might also reverse that proposition and speak of the power that the lover exercises on the beloved. Both are true, and both are part of the picture of God that emerges when the "Galilean vision" is taken with the seriousness it merits.

With respect to men and women, too, there has been a tendency to portray their nature in ways that hardly do justice to that vision. For the point of the vision is that in Jesus we are enabled to discern not only what God is and what God is up to, but also what human beings are moving toward as their end or goal—to become lovers who reflect the divine Love. In order for men and women to be able to become such lovers, the materials of which they are made, the basic stuff of human nature, as we may phrase it, must be good. Of course it has been tragically disordered; humankind has deviated very far from the proper path of its "becoming." But the potentialities that are humanity's by creation are good in themselves and may be used for the good. Otherwise the biblical insight that God saw that it was very good, spoken about the world as a whole and humankind in particular, is rendered null and void.

Nonetheless, much theology has taken humankind to be a *massa corruptionis* (a corrupted mass), sunk in a depravity which is so total that its whole being is evil—a position which even John Calvin did not intend but which some of his successors have gloomily asserted to be a correct portrayal of humanity —and which can be put right only by a miracle of the sort that does not renew and restore but rather replaces it by something entirely different. In reaction to this appalling picture, other theologians have been very cheerful about humanity and have taught in Pelagian fashion that humankind's own efforts, plus the divine concern for humankind, will in and of themselves bring humanity to God's intended goal. Both pictures by themselves are false, as our discussion up to this point has shown. If we need something of the realism of the former picture, we also need something of the optimism of the latter; and the way to such a comprehensive view is by emphasizing both humankind's imaging of God and its failing by willful choice to assume the divine likeness. Men and women can indeed become the lovers they were meant to be; but to become so they need the lure, the pressing solicitation, and the strength found in a love that will never let them go, a love that is nothing other than Love as divine, as God. They are free to respond to or to reject that Love.

We know nowadays that ours is a world that is dynamic, in movement or process. We know its societal or organic nature, and we know that any portrayal of God or humankind in such a world must be equally dynamic and societal. Failure here is patently a denial of the facts about humankind, especially as we have come to understand it in the light of more than a hundred years of biological, psychological, and sociological investigation. Failure here also makes the divine a meaningless concept, alien to the world's experience and unable to include within it that richness of social life which is so obvious to us and important for us. We must see God as the living and loving God; we must see humankind as in the making, not as a finished article. All this has its profound implications for the question of ethics.

Two factors are of special significance. One is the Christian conviction that what I have consistently styled "the way the world *really* goes" or "the grain of the universe" is *not* on the side of the biggest battalions, even if at any given moment or for some period of time this may seem to be so. On the contrary, the dynamic thrust of the universe, at its deepest level, is toward shared good and is essentially the power of love. Heaven and earth may pass away, to be sure; and we must face up to the finite nature of the particular style of creation known to us in this cosmic epoch—"the form of this world is passing away" (1 Cor. 7:31). But the conviction remains that God has resources, primarily those of loving concern, which enable God to continue the work of love, in another style of creation if you will, and always to receive and to use the good that has been accomplished in any and every created order. Thus there is a cosmic backing for human efforts after decency, mutuality, and the common life.

The second factor has to do with human freedom. However limited that freedom is by circumstances, however partial its manifestations may be in particular situations, whatever may be the necessities that time and place impose, there *is* in human beings a capacity to choose and a liberty in choosing. For the most part this may show itself in the little day-by-day decisions, although there are occasions when momentous decisions are possible and necessary, involving vast numbers of people. Such freedom carries with it, moreover, the responsibility which free agents are bound to assume for the decisions that they make and the actions that implement those decisions. Thus I must ask myself again and again whether this or that supposedly insignificant choice, with this or that apparently unimportant act following upon the choice, does or does not contribute to the wider good. I must ask myself if I am deciding for a course that can bring more truly personal existence to others or to another, or whether the decision I make is for my own self-satisfaction and self-interest and nothing more. I must ask myself whether I am making any contribution, be it small or great, to the ongoing of the purpose of shared life in the world. And this means that I am asking myself whether I am willing to be a "co-worker with God," what Whitehead (perhaps even more profoundly) was prepared to style "co-creator with God."

Now an ethic that has this sort of background and works itself out in this kind of context is going to be quite different from one that talks about God in terms of power and about people in terms of slavish obedience to absolutely unalterable laws which are imposed upon them entirely from outside. It is also very different from an ethic which assumes that God is primarily a moral dictator who sets up rules bearing little relationship to people's own concrete nature and their ongoing movement toward realization (or lack of realization) of genuine possibilities. In that sort of ethic, people are indeed expected to behave in slavish obedience. Their dignity has disappeared and their integrity has been destroyed. No wonder there has been a violent reaction to it on the part of those who have discovered the joy of living in some measure of freedom, the zest of adventure in a world that is not fixed or closed but is open to novelty, the terrible sense of failure when one is not cooperating in a deep cosmic movement toward good, and the exhilarating sense of achievement when one is thus cooperating.

It would be quite wonderful if those whose professional concern is with ethical issues would seek to work out, as fully as possible, the implications of this newer slant. Some are doing just this, to be sure; but the unfortunate impression still remains that the representatives of the Christian tradition are interested only in maintaining the status quo or even worse the status quo ante. Yet if anything is clear to us, it is that in this world we cannot continue in some fixed position. Either we go forward or we lose out. It is impossible to go backward. But we can read the signs of the times, learn from them, and do everything in our power to preserve whatever was valuable in our human past while we move on to what promises to be valuable in the future. This requires courage, imagination, and willingness to take risks. It also demands hard thinking and great effort. Some of us, even if in our years we are old, are sure that this is worth doing—and perhaps not surprisingly, it gives a peace that is not above and beyond all striving but right there in the midst of our striving. For peace is not merely the absence of war but, as Professor Macquarrie has so nobly urged upon us, the wholeness of life that brings satisfaction and joy in living.

Appended Note on "Law"

Appended Note on "Law"

It has been suggested that despite my comments in the course of the lectures that (with revision) form the chapters of this book, I have not made sufficiently clear the attitude I take about law and laws. I have stressed the absolute centrality of love as *the* ethical principle, it is said, but I have not indicated the necessary place for social norms, which are essential if any community is to exist in an orderly and patterned way. After all, the emphasis on love seems to carry with it the corollary that each person can and will act in a fashion which seems to him or her appropriately loving, without recognizing that in the broader realm of impersonal relationships some imposed standards are necessary. Furthermore, not everyone is capable of planning behavior in terms of the loving decision; only the sophisticated, on the one hand, or the genuinely devoted, on the other, can be expected to order themselves by that kind of ethic.

I had thought that my discussion of the place of guidelines would have handled most of these problems, but evidently this is not the case. Hence I shall attempt in this brief note another statement of the position that I believe the emphasis on the absolute ethic of love entails with respect to rules or law.

In the first place, I have protested against antinomianism—the idea that *no* abiding principles exist. Certainly *one* principle does exist, and that is love itself. But by the same token love requires implementation in concrete actions. Nobody can love in the abstract; to talk as if one could is to parody love and to make it so general and vague that it has no cutting-edge. If I am to act lovingly, I must act toward this person, in this situation, under these circumstances, and with this or that objective in view. Hence there is unquestionably the need for what in a different context John Bennett has taught us to call "middle axioms"—secondary principles, as we might put it, that will provide the ways in which the absolute may be adapted to the particular conditions in which human beings live their lives.

Such middle axioms are not to be given the position of true absolutes, with the right to equally absolute obedience. In other words, they are not like love itself, with its totally binding demand. Neither are they like imposed regulations enforced by some supposed authority on pain of severe penalties when they are violated.

Of course it is necessary to have agreed standards, such as traffic regulations or requirements for honest advertisement of wares by manufacturers and business firms. Nobody has ever claimed that these standards have an absolute quality; they are convenient ways of making it possible for people to get around a town or city or countryside, in the first instance, or to know what they are being offered as commodities, in the second instance. The laws for the regulation of traffic might very well be altered and frequently *are* altered; the standard of accuracy in advertisement may vary from time to time with due regard for the nuances of meaning that may be read into, or out of, public announcements.

Furthermore, some kind of determination of, say, the mode of public recognition of marriage is evidently necessary; hence the several states of the American union have their marriage laws. And there must be enforcement of regulations with respect to entry into people's houses, the transfer of possessions, the maintenance of public order so that it will be safe for citizens to walk the streets without fear of attack by thieves or gangsters, and the like. But none of these is supposed to have divine sanction, so that a violation of them constitutes at the same time an outrage against "how the universe goes." They are mostly matters of convenience, and they depend for their persistence on the consent of the great majority of those who live in a given community or state.

But this is very different from the idea that there is a set of laws imposed from on high, in all their detail, failure to follow which is a matter of eternal concern. My protest against the so-called law ethic was simply a way of insisting that there are in fact no such eternal laws, only the law of love. Everything else is secondary and subject to change under different circumstances and with respect to different problems that people must face and handle.

This is not to say, on the other hand, that we can reject with easy conscience what I have styled the wisdom of our ancestors. Those ancestors did attempt to work out a viable series of corollaries of fundamental righteousness, which at bottom is itself the working out of the requirement for love—that is, mutuality and sharing—which constitutes the one absolute. The laws that they proposed were not entirely arbitrary; they were intended, perhaps unconsciously, to promote the general good of the people to whom they were directed. What is required of us is to see that this was the case, and then also to recognize that the guidelines, to use the term I suggested in the preceding chapters, are always to be given serious consideration. This is not because in and of themselves they are absolute, of course; rather, it is because they provide the present generation with indications of how in the past men and women felt that the great absolute of love working through righteousness might be implemented in actual practice.

Nor do these guidelines stand precisely in the same status as they once may have had. They require some sort of interpretation under new circumstances. The Old Testament's ten commandments, for example, cannot be applied to contemporary conditions without just such interpretation. The whole enterprise of casuistry, both in Judaism and in Christianity, has been concerned to develop this interpretation. What exactly does adultery, forbidden in the ten commandments, really indicate as wrong? How widely can this idea be applied, under what circumstances and in what situations? Again, "bearing false witness" or lying seems plain enough. But is it? To what degree does it permit withholding truth for the sake of some presumed greater good? In what sense am I supposed always and everywhere to say exactly what I believe to be the case, if and when others may be seriously damaged by my saying it?

This kind of question shows that the matter of obedience to law is not as simple as some have assumed it to be. Nonetheless, the total impact of the ten commandments is to show that there is a necessity in human affairs for men and women to be honest, to be decent in relations with one another, to have some understanding of the commitments made in, say, marriage, and the like. And the reason is that only thus can mutuality be found. Precisely *how* these needs will be worked out is not easy to say; different people, at different times and in different places, will have different ways of doing this.

Yet the end or object that is sought in all such orderings is exactly the mutuality or sharing in the common life which is the imperative of love-in-action. And because this point has so often been forgotten in conventional discussions of ethical issues, I have felt it necessary to put my stress *there*. Once that point has been accepted, other questions will follow. But unless it is accepted, the truly *human*, and hence the divinely purposed, meaning of ethics has been forgotten.